Also by Dr. Phil McGraw

LIFE
CODE

BY Dr. Phil McGraw

THE NEW RULES FOR
WINNING IN THE REAL WORLD

Published in Los Angeles, California, by Bird Street Books, Inc.

ISBN: 978-0-9854627-3-4

Cover Design: Hagop Kalaidjian
Interior Design: Maureen Forys, Happenstance Type-O-Rama

In memoriam of my mother, Jerry McGraw:
a loving mother, grandmother, and great-grandmother, who
joined our Lord on June 17, 2011.

She was an inspiration in life and in death and is
sorely missed but lovingly remembered. And in honor of the
never-ending cycle of life: dedicated to my grandchildren,
Avery Elizabeth and London Phillip.

The anecdotes in this book are used to illustrate common issues and problems that I have encountered, and do not necessarily portray specific people or situations. No real names have been used.

As with all books, this one contains opinions and ideas of the author. It is intended to provide helpful and informative material on the subjects addressed in the publication. It is sold with the understanding that the author and publisher are not engaged in rendering medical, health, psychological or any other kind of personal professional services or therapy in the book. The reader should consult his or her medical, health, psychological or other competent professional before adopting any of the concepts in this book or drawing inferences from it. The content of this book, by its very nature, is general, whereas each reader's situation is unique. Therefore, as with all books of this nature, the purpose is to provide general information rather than address individual situations, which books by their very nature cannot do.

The author and publisher specifically disclaim all responsibility for any liability, loss, or risk, personal or otherwise, which is incurred as a consequence, directly or indirectly, of the use and application of any of the contents of this book.

Acknowledgments

I first thank my beautiful wife, Robin, who has been by my side for 40 years as we've faced down all the "bad guys" together and loved up all the "good guys," always remaining thankful that our true and loyal friends have outnumbered the "bad guys" by a country mile! We have been blessed individually and as a couple to have so many wonderful people in our lives across so many years.

To our sons, Jay and Jordan, you are the reasons your mother and I have strived so hard to understand how to survive and succeed in the real world. Thank you for making us proud by becoming the excellent young men you are: Jay, as an outstanding son, father to Avery and London, and husband to your wonderful wife, Erica; and Jordan, as a wonderful son and talented and deeply passionate musician. If the two of you represent our future, then our world is truly blessed. Thanks for always believing in your ol' dad. It helps me to "keep my feet moving," so as to never let you down.

Thank you, Bob Asahina, for your work on organizing, editing, and researching for this book. Your passion for this project was so obvious and made me know I was on the right track from our very first meeting. Thank you, also, for stimulating me to dig deep, both professionally and personally, for the content within its pages. You made this book better every time you touched it. You are the consummate professional and so much fun to work with!

I acknowledge and deeply appreciate my friend and colleague G. Frank Lawlis, Ph.D., A.B.P.P. (a double diplomate), a fellow of the American Psychological Association and chairman of the advisory board for the *Dr. Phil* show. Thanks for all you have shared and for being at my side personally and professionally for almost 40 years, including your invaluable input on the research, clinical, and content aspects of *Life Code.*

I am also grateful for the valued opinions and editorial input of one of the most respected psychological experts in the world: John T. Chirban, Ph.D., Th.D., clinical instructor in psychology at Harvard Medical School and core faculty member at the Cambridge Hospital. John, thanks for the endless hours of careful review and thoughtful and challenging feedback. You made me and this book better by your comments and by allowing me to see you as a father to your wonderful children over the years.

Thanks to Scott Madsen, who is always deserving of acknowledgment and my deep appreciation for all you do. Thank you, in particular, for your feedback on this book and for running interference and keeping the "hounds" from my door when I was deep in "book mode!"

Carla Pennington, you are truly at the heart of my *Dr. Phil* team, and I thank you for your uncompromising commitment and dedication at my side as we work with so many challenging and deserving stories, many of whom inspired the messages in these pages. I also appreciate your valuable insights and contributions to this book. You always find a way to get it all done when it comes to our work.

Thank you also to Angie Kraus, Melissa Key, Kathy Giaconia, and Barbara Robinson, for your unwavering support, loyalty, and passion. I am grateful for your careful reading and study of this manuscript and for sharing your heartfelt reactions from the first draft forward. You will see your comments and reactions reflected throughout. And thank you, Justin Arluck, for your feedback and for coming up with the acronym BAITER.

Thanks to Bill Dawson, my trusted friend and "foxhole buddy," for encouraging me to always search deep into my thoughts, feelings, and experiences that have enlightened me about the real world and how it works. So much of what I have learned and shared here was experienced as we "fought them off" together in courthouses coast to coast and border to border. As we always say, "Death to the enemy!"

And a very special thanks to Lisa Clark and the entire team at Bird Street Books. Lisa, you don't seem to have the word "no" in your vocabulary and apparently never sleep, eat, or go home! Thanks for caring and finding something special in the manuscript every time you read it and reread it.

Of course, thank you, Oprah, my dear and valued friend, for creating the opportunity and platform for *Dr. Phil*. Had I not met you, I would still be Dr. McGraw, not "Dr. Phil," and this book would never have been written. You continue to be an inspiration, and my family and I are grateful for you every day.

To Jan Miller, Shannon Marven, and my team at Dupree Miller & Associates, Inc., I give my sincere thanks. You are a tireless, committed, remarkable group, and you always go far above the call of duty on all of my literary projects.

Contents

A Behind-the-Scenes Introduction to the New "Life Code"

Even though this is the first page you are reading, I will confess to you that it is the last thing I am writing as I put this book together. I really couldn't have done this introduction justice until the book was finished, because the writing of it has affected me in a meaningful way. To be candid, I usually feel tired and beat up after writing a book, but I don't now. I feel energized and razor sharp about the subject matter. To say that I'm proud of this book would be an understatement. It has been written from a place of passion, determination, and concern. Given my profession and what I have dealt with every day for 35 years, I can unequivocally say I have seen the Good, the Bad, and the Ugly of life. It's in that "seeing" that I have gained what has, at times, been a painful wisdom that I seek to share in the following pages.

In this book, I intend to help you understand *how the world really works* and *who you really are* as you go about dealing with this *real world*. I don't even want you to change who you are so much as I want to *add* to who you are—unless, of course, you are one of the people I am describing in Chapters 1, 2, and 3! I say that because in the first three chapters, you're going to read about the people in your life who would just as soon cheat, exploit, and betray you as they would look at you. When you are done with that part of the book, those people will never be able to sneak up and "blindside" you ever again. Then, we shift gears in a big way, and you're going to read about yourself and get an insider's knowledge-based "Life Code" playbook on how to power up and win, and I mean win big, in your life, regardless of your encounters along the way with any of the "jerks" from the first part.

I want to share every part of the process with you because there's a lot of value in how I developed these "New Rules." When I decided to write about those people in this world who you wish would have never darkened your doorway, I started with my own personal life and experiences. I sat down at my desk at home on a Sunday afternoon and made a list of the people throughout the span of my life who, in my opinion, have sought to hurt me, betray me, and take advantage of me and those I love. Unfortunately, I had a pretty substantial list that spanned all the way from my childhood until this past Christmas! I was so consumed with the process that I forgot to eat, and for me, that is a serious omission!

Here is how I actually went about getting focused. I created a sheet on every single one of these jerks. (Some took several sheets to really capture the "essence" of who they were and what they had done or tried to do! I'm sure some of yours will too.) At the top, I described the scenario wherein they tried to jerk me around. Then, I did kind of an "autopsy" on what had happened in pretty good detail. I identified and listed what they had said and done when they had me in their sights. Hindsight truly is 20/20, so it was not hard to see. As I said, I had a whole set of lists, and I actually put them up on the office wall so I could pace back and forth as I looked for, studied, and added to the commonalities. I even color-coded certain things with my little granddaughter Avery's highlighters so I could see whether certain tactics, certain underhanded dealings, recurred from situation to situation.

Boy, oh boy, was I shocked! The similarities between people who had sought to exploit me in different ways, at different times in my life, were huge. I mean, it was incredible how consistent some of these behaviors and patterns were when compared side-by-side. Remember, I'm talking about people who, in most cases, didn't even know each other. It wasn't as if they had gotten together and attended the same "how to screw people over" class. But somehow or another, they all seem to have similar traits, characteristics, and tactics. This may seem intuitively obvious, but trust me—it wasn't, at least not at first. I didn't just list generalities, like they lied through their teeth. I deconstructed their ploys and tied early behaviors (such as "grooming") to later acts, and so on. I also looked at *who* they were, not just *what* they did.

As I peeled back the layers, I discovered that what these types of people do can be identified and described in a definable, observable fashion and put on a finite list. I could not believe, when I looked at what they had in common, how amazingly similar these jerks are in the ways that they use and abuse people. It jumped out at me like a neon sign, blinking in my face. I stood there thinking, "Are you kidding me? How could I be in this profession this long, get this old, and not have figured out and articulated this before now?" I was livid with myself.

Next, I started scrubbing the literature. I wanted to know whether anybody else had ever tried to figure this out and put it all together in one place. I went to bookstores, Amazon.com, the psychological/psychiatric literature, and the sociological literature. I scrubbed the current Diagnostic and Statistical Manual

(DSM) that lists all the different mental illnesses and syndromes along with detailed traits and characteristics. It is great for what it is, but it distinguishes *differences* rather than commonalities. In short, I came up with zip. Zero.

Maybe authors and researchers were thinking that such an endeavor was too negative, unwieldy, or just indescribable. But come on! We have a world infected with a fungus of certain human beings whose primary purpose in life is to get up every day and take advantage of others, and *who* these people are, and *how* they do what they do, is knowable. It's knowable! And if it's knowable, then it should be avoidable. We can at least take away the element of surprise.

So, later in this book, I'm going to tell you about what I call the "Evil Eight"—the eight identifying characteristics that are dead giveaways when you see these people coming down the pike. If you're like me, when I first saw this information put together in plain language, all in one place, you may hit yourself in the forehead with the heel of your hand and say, "It's so obvious now! Man, oh man, if I had known then what I know now, some things in my life would have been a whole lot different." Well, you're about to know, and things *are* going to be different.

But, I didn't stop there. I did exactly the same process with regard to the good guys. I was on a roll now! I listed those people in my life whom I admire and look up to and have enough intimate knowledge about to really know how they do what they do. These are people whom I have seen succeed, overcome, conquer, and contribute to this world. At the risk of sounding egotistical, I even included myself on that list, because I am proud of my family and my career and my spiritual life. I've been happily married almost 40 years with two great and thriving sons, so I figured, hey, take a look back! At the top of the sheet, I wrote down why I was including a particular person. Their successes spanned business, family and spiritual leadership, and athletics. I included successful people from all walks of life, males and females, young and old, rich and poor; but every single one of them was, at least in my view, a winner in some significant way.

Then, I started making the list of their traits, characteristics, and behaviors just as before. What is it that this person does that has contributed to their success? Education? Intelligence? Commitment? Passion? Social skills? Risk-taking? Analytical skills? Was it their strategy of problem solving or maybe their negotiating skills, philosophy, or coping skills? I put these up on a different wall in the same room. (I was driving Robin crazy!) Again, I started going through and color-coding to see whether there were similarities or whether these were a bunch of unique people who shared little or nothing with others who were also successful. Again, I was shocked! Even though these people came from different walks of life and might never have even heard of each other, the commonalities were incredible. There were differences, certainly, but more importantly, the core list of traits and characteristics, strategies, and styles shared by all of these people was overwhelmingly clear. Success doesn't happen by accident; people don't just get "lucky." Success is *created*, and, just as importantly, once obtained, it must be managed and protected. I didn't see a single success story in which the person at the center, the hero, the victor, didn't come under some attack at some point. You've heard the saying "It's lonely at the top," and it's true.

To say I was excited is a huge understatement. All of these people's formula for success, just as with the bad guys mentioned earlier, was knowable. It was definable and observable and could be put on a finite list. And, believe me when I tell you, this was not a commonsense list. This was not a list that you would easily come up with if you sat down to speculate about what was at the core of their successes. But the good news is, even if not commonsensically obvious, success leaves footprints. You can track success and figure out what is at its core. So, I did the same thing that I did with the other list. I went to the bookstore, I scrubbed Amazon.com, and I got into the psychological, psychiatric, and sociological literature to see whether anyone had done what I was doing. I found a lot of "rah-rah" motivational-type books, tapes, and programs (some pretty good ones, actually, as far as they went), but I did not find one example of anybody talking about how to win in the *real world* and how to *protect* that success once you have it. They talked about things like vision and purpose, but nobody talked about how the *world really works* and how sometimes you have to invent a way and fight the battles.

Now maybe, just maybe, I live in a completely different world than they do, but in my world, cheaters do sometimes win, the early bird doesn't always get the worm, and doing unto others as you wish they would do unto you doesn't always get you what you want, need, or deserve. It makes good copy, it's a good story to tell, and it's how we all *wish* the world was, but it is not the world I live in, and I'm telling you it's not the world *you* live in. To win in the real world, these people I studied became "street smart" and didn't take any "wooden nickels." They didn't sell out their integrity, they didn't settle for what they didn't want, and they played to win.

I have written seven other books and am proud of every one of them. As I said, writing a book is a lot of work. If you're really going to do it right, it takes a lot of time and effort and a really dedicated team. I don't know how other authors do it, but, with me, sometimes a chapter will go through 20 or 25 drafts before being locked, and that's after what might be months of research. Because of that reality, I hadn't been at all sure that I wanted to write another book right now—that is, until I started covering my office walls with all of this information. Once I did that, I became a rabid man on a mission, and this book started to write itself. Robin would come in and say, "Why aren't you complaining about all the work and time this is absorbing?" I said, "Sit down and let me tell you about this book." About ten minutes later, she laughed and said, "Calm down, I get it! I get it."

So, maybe I've told you more than you want to know about where this book came from and how I went about putting it together. But I just thought I would "pull back the curtain" and let you see behind the scenes of everything that led up to what you are about to read. I'm excited about writing it, and I'm excited for you that you are about to read it. Like I said, I'm going to tell you about the "Evil Eight" identifying characteristics of the bad guys, and then I'm going to tell you about what I call the "Nefarious 15" tactics that these people use to get to you and me and everybody else they target. I'm going to show you their secret "playbook;" I'm going to show you exactly, precisely how they do what they do. That knowledge is going to be amazingly empowering to you. And then, we're going to stop talking about the bad guys and start talking about *you*, and I'm going to give you what I call the "Sweet 16"—the 16 things that the successful people who I have studied consistently do to win. And these "Sweet 16" things are things you can do, too. I don't want to change who you are; I want to *add* to who you are and to what you know.

If up until this point you've been doing everything "by the book" but your life still isn't where you want it, you've been reading the wrong book. It's time to read the right one.

Here we go.

Part 1

The Real-World "Bad Guys":
How to Spot and
Defeat Them

1

Life Is a Game: Be a Player or Be Played

"Better to be awakened by a painful truth than lulled to sleep by a seductive lie."

—DR. PHIL McGRAW

Have you ever sat around and wondered how and why someone who you are certain does not have your brains, personality, value system, work ethic, commitment, motivation, or skills often seems to wind up at the top of the heap—while you're stuck in the middle, or even the bottom? Or are you baffled by how your best friend always seems to get all of the attention—while you stand on the sidelines? Or are you amazed by how your sister always manages to end up with the good-looking, popular guy—when you wish he had chosen you instead? Or do you wonder why, after you've had an argument with someone, you're inevitably the one who always feels guilty and apologizes when you know, *I mean really know,* that you did nothing wrong?

Worse still, have you wondered why that guy in the next cubicle, who you *know* to be a backstabbing, brown-nosing, manipulating, "sycophant suck-up," got the promotion or credit that *you* deserved? Or why you get taken advantage of and flat-out betrayed by the very people you trusted and *thought* were your friends and allies? Or why your child is always the one getting bullied at school? Or why someone suckered you, once again, by selling you something you didn't need, at a price you couldn't afford, or by borrowing (taking) your hard-earned money with some sob story and never paying it back? Or why you lost your husband to someone everyone *but* your husband (duh!) knows to be a scheming gold digger? Worst of all, do you ever wonder why people get away with lying, stealing, cheating, or emotionally or physically abusing someone you know and love, or even *you*?

Whether these things happen to you or to someone you care about, you can change *all* of it. Seriously, you can. I'll tell you right now, one goal of this book is for you to stop being victimized and start being "victim-wise!"

If you have had any (or all) of the thoughts I began this chapter with—and I think we all have at one time or another—your "questions," your "wonderings," were very likely statements of frustration and complaint more than they were actual queries. But they *should* be real questions, because they have *real answers*. Answers I'm going to give you. I'm going to tell you the "unvarnished" truth about how and why these things happen to you or those you love so deeply. I'm going to tell you with the honesty and clarity that you have come to expect from me. I'm going to give you the straight truth, nothing less, because knowledge is power, and you can use that power to change the *rest* of your life. Notice I said "the *rest* of your life." I'm a pragmatist; I only want to talk about what you have a chance to change, because that's the only part you should put energy into. It doesn't do any good to just sit around being upset about it if you don't make the effort to figure out what, how, and why it happened. You can be madder than the snake that married the garden hose, but that won't change reality. To do that, you have to get street-smart savvy and recognize that the world rewards *action*.

I'm going to give you the straight truth, nothing less, because knowledge is power, and you can use that power to change the rest of your life.

I want you to learn the actions required to get *and keep* what you want in your life, for yourself and those you love. I want you to learn the new "Life Code" and have a crystal-clear view of how the world *really* works. It all begins with you surrounding yourself with the right people—the good and authentic people—and "unsurrounding" yourself with the wrong people. And we both know there are plenty of *wrong* people in this world. I guess a lot of things in life boil down to the war of good versus evil, and your life and mine are often the battleground. Edmund Burke said, "In order for evil to flourish, all that is required is for good men to do nothing." By the end of this book, I think you will be much better prepared to do "something"—to fight to procure and protect what you value and, if you are a parent, to prepare your children to self-protect when they go out into this "full-contact" world.

Okay, enough generalities. Let's get very real about the world we live in and the challenges and obstacles we all have to contend with and overcome.

I made a threshold decision as I began working on this book. I cannot do it, or you, justice if I'm not willing to share some very personal thoughts, beliefs, values, and heretofore distinctly private experiences. That needs to start right now, so here are some critical truths I have come to understand about me and my very personal point of view as I go about living in this contemporary world: I love life, but not everything in it. I love people, but not all of them. I love myself, but not everything about me. There is a dark side to most things in this world, including life, people, and self, and it is pivotally important to "light up" that dark side and understand those who are controlled by it. It is time to take away the mystery and overcome the denial of its existence, even its existence within ourselves. Understand when I say "dark side," I'm not necessarily talking about "evil" in the spiritual sense, at least not *just* in the spiritual sense. Life experiences, mental illness, drugs, greed, environment, and poor role-modeling can all forge damaged people and can generate a darkness, an exploitiveness, in the way they approach life. Whatever their genesis, there are people in your life (and mine) who will hurt you if you let them.

Getting What You Want and Keeping What You Get

Firstly, I want to show you how you can protect yourself from getting hurt by the damaged and dangerous people lurking around the corner. Hurt by people who live on the dark side, dispense pain as a matter of course, and never shed a tear or give a second thought to how they have victimized you—and may even brag about it. You know I'm right; there are some bad people in this world and in all of our lives.

Secondly, as I said earlier, I plan to give you this new "Life Code," which is defined by new or, in some cases, improved awareness, skills, and attitudes, not just for surviving, but also for winning and winning *big*. This "Life Code" is not just for *getting* what you want but also for *keeping* what you have worked so hard for, including material things and, even more importantly, a fulfilling and peaceful life. There are endless opportunities and possibilities in our current world, and I hope you're as passionate and excited about those opportunities as I am.

I love life, but not everything in it. I love people, but not all of them. I love myself, but not everything about me.

We really do live in exciting times! But for some reason, our society teaches us things like how to read, how to add and subtract, what chemicals make up what substances, who was President over the past 200+ years, and a lot of other facts—but *not* how to win and *not* how to effectively get *and* keep what you want for yourself and your family. Most people in America have a high-school education, but I have not found many curricula that focus on human nature and why we do what we do and don't do what we don't do. You see, those are different skills, skills that require finesse, and are sometimes much harder to describe and teach than a factual formula, for example. But you need this information; we all do. Just because it's hard to articulate doesn't make it any less critical to have.

I have spent my professional and personal life studying exactly that and specifically studying success and how to not only have it but how to sustain it. Analyzing what it takes to win and win big in life has been a passion that has defined much of who I am. I have had so much fun doing this that I'm bursting to share it with you. By learning and applying this new "Life Code," you will not believe how your life can and will change.

Analyzing what it takes to win and win big in life has been a passion that has defined much of who I am.

Think about it: If you take flying lessons, you can learn to fly; swimming lessons, you can learn to swim; singing lessons, you can learn to sing. So, why not take winning lessons? Why not figure out what to think, feel, and do in order to get what you want for yourself and your family? We live in a different world, and it requires different skills and knowledge than it did even ten years ago. At the risk of sounding cocky, if you read this book and others don't, you are going to have a huge "leg up" on the competition. They will be either embracing a mind-set that no longer fits our fast-paced, changing world or, more likely, just passively accepting whatever comes their way, maybe good, maybe bad. You, on the other hand, are going to have a well-thought-out, passion-fueled strategy built on the skills and confidence that stem from rolling up your sleeves and learning what others simply don't know.

You have to start by getting very "real" about who you are, including your strengths and weaknesses, *and* getting real about how the world *really* works, both the good and the bad. And it's a rapidly changing world, so it takes commitment to keep up.

Some experts estimate that we at least double our knowledge base every two years! Technology is the best example. When I was in high school, I had barely even heard of a computer; now we can't live without them. I used rotary-dial phones, not cell phones. I never saw *Pong* until college, let alone video games! Kids weren't one click away from a bottomless pit of pornography and didn't interact with strangers in some "chat room" on the World Wide Web. Much of what your parents told you about the world simply doesn't apply anymore or just won't cut it in this day and time, not because they wanted to mislead you but because it has radically changed since you left the nest. Back then, there was no Internet pounding on you, no transient lifestyle destroying your neighborhood lifestyle, no cable television bombarding you with glamorized sex and violence—and there were, at least seemingly, fewer scammers and exploiters out there seeking to take advantage. You didn't have all of those influences and factors to contend with, but you do now and, of critical importance, so do your children. Soooo, let's get current. Let's get tuned in to what it *does* take in this day and time to build the life you want.

It isn't just knowledge or technology that has changed. Yesterday's rules and expectations about relationships, emotions, and interacting simply don't apply anymore, at least not like they once did, and those who figure that out and adapt to the current world will have an incredible edge. There are all kinds of people in this world, ranging from the sheltered, naïve, "goody two-shoes" neophytes to the street-smart, savvy, worldly people who are tough and smart. I want that to be you. I want you to be tough and smart when you need to be.

I've lived on both sides of that dichotomy, and trust me, being smart and tough is better, way better. But I'm so excited about "powering you up" that I'm getting ahead of myself. Power begins with having a crystal-clear view of reality and what each and every person in your life is driven by. That will take a bit of a "wake-up" call because we typically choose to be blind to such things as why people do what they do. For some reason, it just seems to be human nature to choose to take people at face value. Yes, that blindness is a choice. You might be wearing rose-colored glasses that are distorting your view of what's really happening around you and to you.

Power begins with having a crystal-clear view of reality and what each and every person in your life is driven by.

So, let's "wake up" and get really clear and up-to-date about an element of society we don't like to think about and wish didn't exist. I'm talking about the people in your life who are negative and exploitive. They are obstacles to your success, happiness, security, and peace of mind. Once you "get" how they think, feel, and act, they become a puzzle that is easily solved. You should know that many people advised me against writing this part of the book, saying that it was too negative and that people don't really want to face the truth or deal with the ugly side of life. Obviously, I said, "Wrong! I'm not writing to a bunch of mouth-breathers here! Do not underestimate my readers, my support-ers, my viewers. We have been getting real together for 15 years, and they *do* want the truth; they do want to know what I know about their world!" It might shock you, it might even horrify you, but most importantly, this knowledge will empower you.

Ask yourself these questions: Do you crave routine? Are you so used to doing, speaking, and thinking the same things day in and day out that you feel, quite literally, like someone else is at the controls and you're just a passenger? I'm here to tell you that there can be real danger in routine. We can become such crea-tures of habit that we go on "automatic pilot" and stop paying close attention to our world. It can seem like a harmless rhythm of life, but *not* paying attention is *never* harmless. We get lulled to sleep by the routine of repetition and predictability. We get bored, get dull, and lose our emotional edge and sensitivity, if we ever had it, and in so doing we can put ourselves and those we love in danger—danger of being preyed upon by those in our lives who are more than happy to swoop in or "seep" in and take what isn't theirs, wreak havoc in our lives, and cause pain. We fall into a stupor of unthinking, an innocent or unmindful trance where we don't react to warning signs, or even clear and present dangers.

It can seem like a harmless rhythm of life, but **not** *paying attention is* **never** *harmless.*

The common mugger on the dark street at night is a good example of how shuffling along on "auto pilot" can land you in trouble. Does he choose the sharp, alert, strong-looking man or woman who has a presence and is glancing around with a keen alertness? Or does he pick the person walking head down, tuned out, and just going through the motions? We can and do get "mugged" in life just as we can get mugged on the street if we shuffle along. Those from the dark side seek the gullible, the trusting, or the inattentive. Almost all of the Internet scams, for example, target the elderly, the lonely, the desperate. They hunt in the neophyte end of the continuum, so if that is where you exist, you may well be getting hunted as we speak.

I wish I had written this book a long time ago. I didn't, though I should have. I'm writing this book now to create an "urgent awareness" within you and a plan to activate it in your life, starting right now. I hope that when you finish this book, you will feel a sense of personal peace and power based on a greater emotional and social competency that makes you anything but an easy target for those who come at you from the dark side. I hope that you feel awake, alert, in-tune, and like you're in the driver's seat as you implement the new "Life Code" in every area of your world.

In spite of all of my extensive and, I think, excellent training, there was a time when I really didn't understand or confront how the world truly worked. I knew how it appeared to work. I learned the traditional lessons about the hydraulics of our lives: Work hard and be rewarded; keep your nose to the grindstone; be honest and loyal; be patient and caring and giving because good things come to those who wait; trust in human nature and give your fellow man the benefit of the doubt; and 1,000 other virtues framed and presented as "good qualities." It all makes for a great story, and as a self-confessed "incurable optimist," I believe in "goodness and light." But sadly, that story is changing, and there is more to it, much more, and the whole story rarely gets told.

The part of the story that needs more telling is the part that alerts us to the fact that embracing those good and wholesome values and qualities, without some major and urgent awareness, can set us up to be abused, exploited, and left in life's "dust." It's part of the story that takes away naïveté and prepares us for a darker side of human nature. It can even be found at our highest levels of academic learning. The leading business schools in the leading universities teach how the banking and financial market systems work (or are supposed to work), but they sure didn't teach how to spot and appropriately deal with self-dealing by major banks and Wall Street firms. That would have been a valuable class!

When you get right down to it, I fear that only some of what I was taught is true all of time, some of it is true some of the time, and some of it isn't true any of the time! The real truth is that much of what we were all taught is not so much how the world *really* works as it is how the world *should* work. In other words, it's how things should be done in "polite" society if everyone has a clear moral compass. But even if the values taught are true and just, and many are, you must be a realist. Be prepared for when those desirable values and beliefs are violated by those who have no moral compass, ignore basic values, and seek to exploit. We need to talk about what *really* happens in marriage, work, society, politics, and even religion. There's an old saying my football coaches used to tell us: "BS the fans, not the players!" I want you to become a player.

> *The real truth is that much of what we were all taught is not so much how the world* really *works as it is how the world* should *work.*

I say "player" because so much of life is a competition. You may wish it wasn't, but it is. It becomes pretty clear if you step back and evaluate it. You competed for your mate, your job, your social position, and your friends. You worked hard to create a family, make a home, and maybe build up a nice little "nest egg." And now you have to fight to protect those things. It seems like we spend the first half of our lives trying to get ahead, creating some stability and building our success, and then we spend the second half just trying to keep people from taking it all away from us. And some of that fight is against people who aren't like you. They will lie, cheat, steal, use, and abuse. They will bully you, molest your children, steal your husband or wife, and take credit for your work. They will sabotage you at every turn. And by the way, they aren't coming; they're already here! They're in your life and mine, maybe even in your own home or family.

My spiritual upbringing taught me to pray for the misguided people in my life, and I always have and always will, and I hope you do the same for those in your life. *But* (and this is a big *but*) praying for them does not mean that we—you and I—shouldn't also protect ourselves and those we love from them. In fact, it's our duty to self-protect because, true to their reptilian nature, these people, like snakes, will inject their venom into us (if not destroy us) without flinching. We must open our eyes to the "games" they play and boldly confront this very negative and unsavory part of our world.

In fact, it's our duty to self-protect because, true to their reptilian nature, these people, like snakes, will inject their venom into us (if not destroy us) without flinching.

In the following chapters, I'm going to tell you how to spot them and neutralize them so you are inoculated against their attacks and how to win this competition for whatever it is that you are fighting. If you think I'm just a cynic; if you're not interested in getting real and acknowledging that there are some truly bad people out there, committing to protecting yourself and your loved ones, and preserving what you earned and value and seek in life; if you want to be average; if you want to sit in the middle of the bell curve and "receive" rather than "create" what comes your way and hope that nobody takes it away from you—then you can stop reading right now, because this book is not for you.

Here is my hope and my promise: I *hope* you let me give you a powerful edge in your life by being willing to learn how you can steel yourself against the dark side of this life and the people who would do you harm. I *hope* you are willing to learn that some of the lessons you've been taught about how to get ahead in this life or find true peace are myths; they are just crocks, plain and simple. We will challenge many timeworn beliefs, and if they withstand challenge, then fine, hang on tight. But if they don't, be prepared to hit the eject button and radically change what you think, feel, believe, and do. I *hope* you power up and start more proactively creating what you want and deserve in this life. And I *promise* that if you do, your head will rest easier on the pillow at night, because you will know that a savvy player (you) stands in the gap, protecting you and your family. Knowledge is power, and I'm offering you some of both right now. "The truth will set you free." I believe that, even if it's, in part, an ugly truth or includes things you don't *want* to hear. A great attitude for reading *Life Code* is: "Sorry to hear it, but *glad* to know it!"

Life Isn't Fair. So What?

Oh, and before we go on, let's get one more thing out of the way. If bad things are happening to you or someone you love, those things are not a result of bad luck. I'm not a big believer in luck. I believe the harder you work, the luckier you get! I don't too much believe in accidents either. For the most part, accidents happen because someone—in my life it's usually me—had to do something stupid, wrong, or careless to enable the "accident" to occur.

I've been a pilot for 40+ years, and during a portion of my career I was involved in accident investigation, especially scheduled airlines. I quickly learned that when a plane crashes, somewhere along the line, somebody had to do something wrong. If everybody did exactly what they were supposed to do, exactly the way they were supposed to do it, 99.9999 percent of the time the plane would not have crashed. Maybe the pilot ignored a bad weather alert. Maybe a mechanic performed a sloppy maintenance check and missed a tiny leak in the hydraulic valve that controls the rudder. Maybe the flight controller was inattentive at the radarscope. And how many car "accidents" result from drivers who are texting at the wheel? Or running a red light? Or simply driving under the influence?

> ### *Knowledge is power, and I'm offering you some of both right now.*

It's no different in interpersonal relationships, whether personal or professional. When you break it down, it's usually not "bad luck." It's not some kind of accident when you get passed over at work, your spouse makes a decision to have an affair (most certainly not your fault, but maybe at least foreseeable if they cheated in their previous three relationships, for example), or you get "screwed" in a business deal. Some people "lose" or come out on the short end because they don't know how the game of life is really played. They don't know, for example, just how low some people can go or how dark they can get.

It is ugly but true that some people, a lot of people, "win" just because they play the game of life according to a different set of rules or no rules at all, and they are very skilled at it. And I'll tell you something else: Simply put, many times those "winners" cheat! They cheat to win, at your expense. On the playground we hear children say "Cheaters never win, and winners never cheat!" Yeah, right! That is the chant of an innocent child. Leave it on the playground, because "that dog don't hunt," as we say in Texas—not in the real world it doesn't.

BAITERS: WHO ARE THEY?

B   Backstabbers

A   Abusers

I   Imposters

T   Takers

E   Exploiters

R   Reckless

So, how do we refer to these people who cheat, exploit, use, and abuse? I think of them as BAITERs (for people who are "Backstabbers/Abusers/Imposters/Takers/Exploiters/Reckless").[1] We will talk in great detail later, but for now, understand that we are talking

---

[1] The BAITERs, as I conceptualize them for the current discussion, are not one-dimensional people who are all exactly alike. They don't all come from an identical background or get to be who they have become based on similar experiences. If this group of people were to collectively present themselves to mental-health professionals for evaluation, they would not all have the same diagnosis and would instead be scattered across several different categories. Some would likely be diagnosed as antisocial personalities, some borderline personalities, and some paranoid personalities. Some might be considered oppositional defiant personalities or a number of other diagnostic categories. Some might fit into multiple diagnostic categories. Some would just be, in my opinion, downright evil. Others might simply be damaged or lacking the proper upbringing, simply not knowing any better. But for the purposes of our discussion, whatever their etiology or diagnostic classification, you will find that certain behavioral patterns and corrupted values show up with great commonality across the group. Religious folks might classify the behavior of BAITERs as "sin," and psychiatry/psychology might call it "sin-drome/syndrome." These labels may be describing different patterns, and sometimes they might overlap.

about people who believe the "means are justified by the end." They are totally self-focused and results-oriented, and they are willing to do anything, absolutely anything, to achieve their goal, whatever it may be—a job, a promotion, money, a wife or husband (maybe even yours), attention, an escape from accountability, or anything else they desire. For most people, of course, "anything" may mean only hard work, smart work, dedication, and commitment. But for BAITERs, it may mean taking a darker approach, where they don't try just to win, but to win at your expense, or where they use you as a stepping-stone or steal your place in the game.

This is an unpleasant picture, I know, but a realistic one nonetheless. As you'll learn in Chapter 2, these people don't see the world the way you do. They do not have your standards for relationships. They lack empathy—the "fellow feeling" that enables human beings to appreciate and identify with another person's emotions. They lack conscience. They lack the ability to feel remorse, and they selfishly and narcissistically pursue whatever their own egos demand. They are, consciously and

---

For the purposes of our discussion, I'm not sure it should matter to you *why* they stole your husband, got your job, attacked your reputation, or stabbed you in the back. My point is that "evil" is real and dangerous and that we need to identify it and deal with it effectively—or we may end up with the short end of the stick. If you appoint yourself to be in charge of "fixing" them, then causal information has a significant bearing, but that's not the purpose of the current discussion. Think about it this way: You're standing on the street in front of your house and somebody drives over your foot and smashes it, breaking several bones and requiring you to have a painful surgery and arduous recovery process. Whether they did it out of carelessness or pure meanness doesn't really change the damage to your foot. That foot is just as smashed either way. So, for the purposes of this discussion, BAITER is a summary term that generally describes those who create pain, heartache, and havoc in your life. We will talk later about forgiveness, and maybe then motivation plays a part, but I'll let you decide that at the time.

subconsciously, unscrupulous. They use dirty tricks and under-handed politics. They exploit, abuse, lie, cheat, and manipulate. They do not hesitate to commit any nefarious act that will take them closer to their goal. They are committed to win and to win at any cost—and that "cost" is often paid by you.

It is ugly but true that some people, a lot of people, "win" just because they play the game of life according to a different set of rules or no rules at all, and they are very skilled at it.

And the truth is that sometimes you actually *help* them hurt you. If you're like a lot of folks in this world, you're probably not sure about exactly what it is that you deserve. Am I really worthy of the promotion? Do I really deserve such a great mate? Can I measure up when the pressure is on? Those doubts and questions and a thousand like them can make you tentative in stepping up and boldly claiming what you want. You might even freeze or "choke" under pressure, even if just for a fleeting moment. But it is that tentativeness, that moment of hesitation or doubt that your competition, particularly the BAITER, seizes upon to get an edge against you.

To me, integrity means doing the right thing even if nobody is watching. But for the BAITERs—the exploiters and abusers—the fact that nobody is watching merely means it's easier for them to operate. They don't even bother trying to find reasons or to rationalize their attitude and moves; they are driven by blind ambition and a cutthroat mentality that they access without a second thought, and you lose.

And sometimes, many times, the BAITERs don't even have to cheat because you default to them by simply not "getting" what is going on. Life is a "full-contact" hard-knocks game even before the cheating starts. These people understand that life is full of negotiating, positioning, influencing, and working the system. You might never pre-arrange to "run into" your boss or your hoped-for mate to get a chance for some critical face time, but they do. They will show up at his church on Sunday and just happen to "bump into" him! "Gee, I didn't know you attended here. I would love it if you could tell me about the place and the people." You may think that is highly manipulative or downright unacceptable, and you'll have plenty of time to think it, because you'll be sitting at home while she's at your job or out with your Mister.

In fact, your competition could be someone who simply outhustles you to win, rather than a flat-out BAITER who lies and cheats. Of course, you have to make a distinction in your life between the two, and this is where intent figures into the equation because that distinction should be based on intent. If someone is deliberately causing you pain or harm or putting you at risk or wantonly disregarding your well-being, that person is most certainly a BAITER. This differs from someone who is just in a conflict with you because your interests are not aligned.

If someone is deliberately causing you pain or harm or putting you at risk or wantonly disregarding your well-being, that person is most certainly a BAITER.

While some people are wondering why life isn't fair, others are seizing, and sometimes stealing, the moment. They're not timid; they steal the attention and strategically position themselves for a chance to win. They are bold enough to step up and ask for what they want and ask again and again until they get it. Meanwhile, others unwittingly just "lie down" and let them have their way.

Am I saying you have to become like "them" to win or even survive? No, of course not, but you *do* have to plug in, engage, and stop letting them abuse you and your trust while you wish that things were different. You do have to play smarter, harder, and better. That means changing what you are doing and how you are thinking.

I'm sorry to have to tell you that right now, I'm 100 percent certain the very people I'm describing, the BAITERs, are in your life and mine and are willing to take advantage of you in some way—even to the point of actively wishing you harm. If that sounds paranoid, I assure you, it is not. The reality is that there are many predatory people out there. So, unless you live in the Pleasantville movie set with Tobey Maguire, you are very likely at risk, at least in some parts of your life. Maybe it's a "friend" or a co-worker or even a family member. Maybe it's a salesman cheating you, a boss abusing you, or a bully picking on you or your child. It may not be fun to face the truth, but it is the truth.

For those of you who are still with me, you might be asking this legitimate question: Does that harsh assessment apply to everyone in your life? No, of course not. The world in general and your personal world in particular are a melting pot that includes a broad array of people, ranging from your biggest and most sincere supporters to the most cold-blooded, selfish, and self-serving BAITER. In a perfect world, dishonest, exploitive behavior would never, ever be rewarded because it is never a good practice to reward bad behavior (which is why we should never give into to our child's tantrums, right?). But you know better. As much as you might not like it, you know that sometimes the world does reward bad behavior.

And you must be aware that it's not just your spouse, neighbor, or co-worker who is potentially "playing" you. There are so many stealthy manipulators in our lives that it's shocking we aren't even more outraged than we are and marching in protest on a daily basis. There is a trillion-dollar-a-year corporate marketing and advertising machine that is programming us, and our innocent children, during every waking moment. The message is we are not okay if we don't buy what they sell, if we are not constant and consummate consumers. Fast-food companies play mind games by selling you "acceptance" rather than food when the commercial focuses on happy, smiling, accepting people eating at the restaurant. They hardly even show the burgers! They did research and learned that you want to feel like you're a *part* of something, like you *belong*, so that is what they sell. Auto companies sell sex and romance with beautiful models and exotic backdrops rather than cars. "Smoke and mirror" Photoshopped models wear the newest fashions on bodies so emaciated they look like walking hangers but are glamorized for our young daughters to emulate and aspire to. Buy our food and be part of this happy scene! Buy our car and be in love and cruising along the ocean shore. Buy our clothes and be like us. Join our club by wearing our label!

There are so many stealthy manipulators in our lives that it's shocking we aren't even more outraged than we are and marching in protest on a daily basis.

And politicians spend billions to research and identify *your* fears so they can then exploit them. Vote for us or your worst fears will come true! And the list goes on and on and on. We *so* need to call them on that manipulative crap! Things are getting worse, not better, when it comes to the science of manipulation. We need to fight back, and it starts with you being "on to them." Remain in denial, and you can guarantee that you'll be taken advantage of by these insidious methods. Or use this book and incorporate this new "Life Code" as your new guide and your wake-up call, and guarantee that you'll be more equipped to fend off such attacks.

Hey, it happened to me! As I'll tell you in detail in Chapter 2, I was once taken advantage of by someone I trusted to handle my financial affairs. Even though it was my business as a psychologist to understand people's behavior, I was completely fooled by this person. Frankly, in retrospect, I was a "Pollyanna," and it cost me and my family a lot of money and heartache. I made the mistake of not listening to my gut.

I can't change what happened in the past, and neither can you. But I have changed what has happened since, and so can you! There was a "death of innocence," so to speak, but that's okay because it is real. Am I bitter? No, I'm not bitter; I'm better.

The Death of Innocence

For America, 9/11 marked a collective, national "death of innocence." Up until that day, we, all of us, heard about acts of terrorism from overseas and wondered how those people lived under such a constant threat. We did not want to even consider that one day it could be us. I mean, come on, this is America, the greatest and most powerful country in the world. No one would dare aggress against us, certainly not here on American soil. But on that tragic day, evil visited our shores. It was a sad national wake-up call. We were forced to consciously acknowledge a threat that had been there all along—that we are hated, actually hated, by hundreds of millions of people the world over. We were forced to go on national alert. We resisted, but we made the attitude and life adjustment and came around.

It's time to do that again, but this time in your own life. You know that what I'm saying is true, and you could probably make a "threats" list right now about people and circumstances in your own life that could cause you pain if you fail to maintain vigil and take protective actions. Maybe it is a kid at school pestering your child to do drugs or a family member or co-worker who you know in your heart is toxic, though you haven't dealt with the situation. I believe we all know the truth when we hear it, even if it is not what we wanted to hear, and we feel better once we come to grips with reality. Think about it. If you are worried about a spot on an X-ray or a rumor that your teenager is up to no good, your friends can pat you on the back of the hand and reassure you, they can tell you what you want to hear, but deep down, don't you know better—or at least *want* to know the truth? Of course you do, because you are smart. My dad used to say, "Boy, there are two things that don't get better with time, bills and problems!" He was right; early acknowledgment and early intervention or action are always best. Denial is childish.

> *I believe we all know the truth when we hear it, even if it is not what we wanted to hear, and we feel better once we come to grips with reality.*

From this point forward, I challenge you to be totally and even brutally honest with yourself. If you are creating problems and fear and anxiety in the absence of any real threat, stop doing that! You don't need to manufacture drama. It can distract you from recognizing and reacting when a very real threat is upon you. Don't buy into either imagined dangers or mindless reassurances of people telling you they "know that everything will be just fine" when you know they haven't a clue what they are talking about and are only trying to make you feel better. They mean well, but it doesn't help. Dealing with reality helps.

This is one of those times. I'm speaking the truth, and you know it. You must become a sophisticated realist. I want there to be as big of a difference between where you are now in your awareness and where you will be when we are done as there is between a wet-behind-the-ears rookie cop and a seasoned, street-smart veteran. Once you are tuned in, plugged in, and in control of your life, you will experience a genuine peace that comes from knowing and dealing with the truth.

Who's Looking Out for You?

I'm betting that you and I probably come from pretty similar backgrounds. I was born and raised in the middle part of this country. I come from a Christian and God-fearing family. I accepted Christ as my personal Savior when I was 13 years old and value that relationship above all others in my life. Robin and I raised our boys in a God-centered home and believe very much in Christian teachings.

But there's something else I believe. I believe in the old adage "Pray to God, but row for the shore." It's the "rowing" that I want to address now. I don't believe we are "passengers" on the "life bus." I think we create our own experiences; we make our own breaks, because I believe God gave us the gift and responsibility of free will. A huge gift! And as the old saying goes, "To whom much is given, much is expected." He gives us opportunities and allows obstacles, and we have to rise to the challenges.

One of my clergy friends loves to tell the old joke—you've probably heard it before—about a man caught in an unbelievable flood. When all his neighbors were running for high ground, he said, "No, I'm staying here—God will save me." Eventually the flood forced him to his rooftop. Rescuers came by in boat after boat begging him to get aboard, but he said, "No, I'm staying here—God will save me." Finally, when the tide rose above the rooftop and as he was floating in the water, he yelled at the heavens, "God, I kept the faith; I thought you were going to save me!" Then the clouds opened up, and he heard a booming voice say, "Hey, I sent you nine neighbors and three rescue boats. What else do you want from me?"

Once you are tuned in, plugged in, and in control of your life, you will experience a genuine peace that comes from knowing and dealing with the truth.

Maybe I'm trying to be your neighbor, and this book could be your rescue boat.

Inoculate Yourself Against Life's Threats—and Study Success

Now, you're probably thinking that all this talk about competition, about life as a "game," is a little distasteful. Of course, we can debate what "winning" really means, and you may even say that if it takes being manipulative and exploitive to "win," if it takes cheating and lying to win, then "No thanks!"—because that isn't really winning. That's fine with me, and I might even agree with you. *But*—and this is another big *but*—you should at the very least know how the game is being played, because, like it or not, you are in it.

If you understand the threat of users and abusers, know how to pick them out of the crowd, and are wise to their methods and tactics, then and only then can you protect yourself and your loved ones.

So don't be put off by the term "game," because it does not refer simply to frivolous things. Many games are very serious, and some games are life and death. You can sit back in self-righteous splendor and say, "Well, Dr. Phil, I just don't play games. I'm not a game-player." I hear you, but you're wrong—you are in the game, you are playing the game, and you cannot *not* choose. Even saying that you don't want to play is a choice. This game is going on around you, and you are in it. All I want you to do is play well.

Think about it: Knowing that someone "cheated" to win will not pay your bills or keep you warm at night if you've been victimized. You may think it's a hollow victory if they used unscrupulous means, but if they get your job or your husband, you're still on your own, and knowing you're "in the right" is little comfort. It has been said that "there are no victims, only volunteers," and I want that to change today! I do not want that volunteer to be you. If you understand the threat of users and abusers, know how to pick them out of the crowd, and are wise to their methods and tactics, then and only then can you protect yourself and your loved ones. You need to know how to counteract them, to stop them in their tracks, *so you don't keep getting "played!"*

Understand, I'm not here to teach *you* how to cheat; I'm here to teach you how *they* cheat. But—and this is important—I'm not asking you to get down to their level. There's an old saying, "When you roll with pigs, you're going to get muddy. And the pigs like it." I'm not here to say you should roll with pigs, but I'm here to prepare you to recognize them when they're coming around the corner and headed into your life.

I'm not here to say you should roll with pigs, but I'm here to prepare you to recognize them when they're coming around the corner and headed into your life.

I will confess to you straight up that some of what I'm going to tell you can be used for evil. It can be used to take advantage of and exploit other people. But so can most things. Pain pills are wonderful if you've had a rough day at the dentist or surgery on your back, but if you abuse them, they can destroy your life. The sun is warm and wonderful and can give you important vitamins to make you healthy, but stay in it too long, and you'll get severely burned. It's not the saw, it's the carpenter.

If there are elements of your life that are missing, I can promise you that it is not always because of what someone did to you or didn't do for you. It is often because of what you do or don't do to create and claim that which you want and need. I want this book to give you tools in the right framework so you can create leverage.

We are ready to move on and get started in earnest. It is time to see the new "Life Code" and "The New Rules for Winning in the Real World." In Chapter 2, I'm going to share with you what I call the "Evil Eight," which are the eight identifiers that can empower you to spot the BAITERs when they enter your space. In Chapter 3, you are going to get the BAITERs' secret "playbook" that includes what I call the "Nefarious 15," the actual tactics the BAITERs use to exploit their targets. Chapter 4 will talk about how to ensure that you don't leave yourself open ever again! Chapter 5 will give you *your* own "Life Code" playbook, including what I call the "Sweet 16" tactics for winning in the real world. Chapter 6 is going to talk about the powerful tool of effective negotiation, and Chapter 7 is all about what you can do as parents to truly prepare your children for living successfully.

Who Are These People?

"Forgive your enemies, but don't forget their names."

—John F. Kennedy

Know (Really Know) Your Adversary, Because They Definitely Know You

I read something in the paper recently that just horrified me. These three men decided to rob a family, so they invaded the family's home. But they didn't just loot the house—they raped the wife, beat the husband, and then killed them both. And the couple's 12-year-old son saw them do it. So what did the criminals do? They caught the boy and drowned him in boiling water.

That's who these people are at their absolute worst, and this is exactly who I am talking about when I refer to BAITERs. Fortunately for all of us, this type of dysfunctional personality and conduct is on a continuum, and those monsters are definitely at the far end in a negative direction. These cruel and violent acts tell you unmistakably that you are dealing with some seriously screwed-up individuals. They are unconscionable and have absolutely no empathy, no regard for human life or the rights of others, and no impulse control. Again, for the purposes of this book, we won't be focusing so much on *why* some people, including these extreme examples, are so sick and demented, as we will on the fact that some of them *are* sick and demented. Regardless of why they are the way they are, the reality is that they live among us—the sick murderers and those who are less violent but highly exploitive. The day this happened, someone was probably standing next to them at the gas station, in line behind them at the fast-food counter, or riding in the same subway car. These are people who make even the staunchest opponents of the death penalty question their stance. When something horrific like that crime happens, we all just shake our heads and say, "I'm sorry, I just don't get it. How could anyone *do* something like that?"

> *Regardless of why they are the way they are, the reality is that they live among us— the sick murderers and those who are less violent but highly exploitive.*

As I say, this kind of dysfunction is on a continuum, and most of us will never run across murderous monsters like that in our lifetimes. But every one of us has had the experience of being caught off-guard by people who are perhaps not so violent but are very much on the dysfunctional continuum. I'm guessing you won't have to think very hard to make a list of the people in your life who have violated you in a variety of ways. Maybe your BAITER wasn't that extreme and violent, but they still inflicted pain and disruption in your life. They betrayed your trust; talked behind your back; seduced your significant other; stole your money; took credit for your work; abused you mentally, emotionally, or physically; controlled, dominated, and isolated you; alienated your friends; or exploited your kindness and goodwill.

Maybe they were your employees who took their pay every day and then stabbed you in the back. Maybe they were employers who used you, abused you, and then unceremoniously fired you. In this world, there are "givers" and "takers," and these BAITERs are takers; in fact, remember that's what the "T" stands for. They can be emotional monsters who are interested in only one person, and that is themselves. They lie, cheat, and steal; use and abuse; and take advantage of the rest of us. By the way, if you ask them, it's *never* their fault, and they *never* feel remorse.

My dad used to say, "There is something about that old boy over there that I just can't stand about me!"

We, of course, are typically left in shock because we weren't prepared, so once again, we just shake our heads and say the same thing: "I never saw that coming. How could they *do* that?" But don't feel bad about not having a natural ability to see them coming. If you don't have larceny in your heart, if you don't approach people and situations looking for an opportunity to exploit, it's very hard to recognize that mind-set in others. We have no construct for it, and we have no experience with it, so it's hard to conceptualize something in others that we haven't experienced within ourselves. That makes us extremely vulnerable.

My dad used to say, "There is something about that old boy over there that I just can't stand about me!" What he was saying is that he could see in others only that which he had to some degree within himself. The converse is true: If we don't have it within ourselves, we can be quite blind to it. That's why I'm working to put these potentialities consciously on your radar screen, so you *can* see them, even though they are foreign to your way of thinking.

If and when this has happened to you, you probably felt very alone. But you don't have to look very far to find others who are in your same boat—and as you know from Chapter 1, I am no exception.

Dr. ~~Phil~~ Pollyanna

I've always been one to believe that it is our responsibility as humans to look for the good in our fellow man and, in fact, not just look for it but actually try to help people be the best they can be. When it turned out that I was going to spend my life in the helping professions, that attitude seemed to lend itself to challenges of my chosen work. And boy, oh boy, did I throw myself into my work. I began working in private practice in clinical psychology and behavioral medicine back in the late 1970s. Between my office hours and an active hospital practice, I worked really hard—too hard, probably. I was a young lion, and I was going to stamp out disease and suffering far and wide! I was going to cure the ills of the world, and I attacked them with a vengeance, sometimes 20 hours a day, day after day. Despite what I now see was a serious lack of balance, my efforts paid off professionally, because I soon had a thriving practice, growing by leaps and bounds.

I knew I couldn't do it alone, so I sought out staff and professionals who seemed to share my passion and would go the extra mile to make a difference. I had a number of other therapists on the team, as well as physicians, technicians, and nurses. Pretty soon, I needed a really strong administrator. Theresa was that person. She was smart, sharp, dedicated, and passionate about working somewhere that was making a difference in people's lives. I met her through her husband, a businessman I knew in town. They had five children, some of whom had been in quite a bit of trouble with the law.

> *I've always been one to believe that it is our responsibility as humans to look for the good in our fellow man and, in fact, not just look for it but actually try to help people be the best they can be.*

Theresa, who physically and personality-wise reminded me of Aunt Bee from *The Andy Griffith Show*, seemed to be a conservative, down-to-earth woman who was "mortified" that her boys had been in trouble. She cried in shame when it came up in any context. She was the choir director at her church, volunteered there several nights a week, and was always more than happy to talk about her faith, and yours. She seemed like a great fit in many ways. But for some reason, I had this nagging feeling in the back of my mind that something just wasn't right. It was not anything I could put my finger on. I thought about it and decided it was *my* problem, not hers. Maybe I was being judgmental about her children. Maybe I felt uneasy because she seemed so much more spiritually developed than me. I mean, come on, I was lucky to get to church once a month, and she practically lived at hers and was constantly ministering to others. I scolded myself and ignored my "gut feeling." I gave her the *benefit of the doubt*. I didn't want to be judgmental, especially based on some vague feeling or because some of her children had been in trouble. I hired her and put her to work.

As it turned out, she came in like a house afire and got things under control. She worked long, hard hours and attended to every detail as if it was her own money and her own business she was handling.

One day, about a year later, I was coincidentally having lunch with her husband. He flew all over the country for business and was in town, so we were catching up a bit. For the first time in my life, I was embarrassingly told by the waiter, "Sir, I'm sorry, but your credit card has been declined. They would like for you to call." I was shocked, embarrassed, and confused. I use credit cards sparingly, but I have never, ever paid one dime of interest because I pay off the balance at the end of every month, so I didn't understand how the card could be rejected. Theresa's husband, sensing my embarrassment, quickly tossed some cash on the table, and we were out of there.

I knew "Aunt Bee" would be all over these idiots in two seconds; how dare they turn down my card! She took this kind of thing personally. They were messing with *her* now! I was right, because she freaked. She felt "horrible" that I had been embarrassed. She blamed herself and could hardly wait to race out of my office and get this fixed.

The nagging feeling I had experienced initially wasn't going away. What was I feeling? Why was I ignoring it? Something just wasn't right. I decided to call Danny, my accountant and long-time good friend, and just chat with him about the whole deal. I knew my books were balanced every month, so it couldn't be that. When I called, they put me on hold while they rounded him up for me. It was in that single moment, sitting there, phone to my ear, that something happened that changed my life forever. It changed my values and challenged my beliefs and my teachings. It changed who I was. I don't understand how it happened to this day. Was it some divine intervention? Dumb luck? A technological glitch? Was it supposed to happen to change who I was or change what I taught others? To prepare me to write this book? I don't know the answer, but I know the impact.

The nagging feeling I had experienced initially wasn't going away. What was I feeling? Why was I ignoring it? Something just wasn't right.

So, what happened that was so life-changing? While I was on hold for Danny, all of a sudden I heard another conversation taking place on my phone, my line! It was like I had "bugged" the other phone line. I was on line 2, and line 3 was the only other line lit up at the time. This had never happened before, and it has never happened since. But on this day, in that moment, another conversation was bleeding over to my line while I was on hold. It was tinny, had a little static, and was electronic sounding, but I could hear it just as plain as day.

What I was hearing on my phone was Theresa on the other line with her husband, whom I had just had lunch with, and he was yelling and screaming at her in an absolute rage. He was calling her every name in the book: "You b----! You lying c---! Are you doing it again? Don't you lie to me! If you're screwing with this man's money, I swear I'll put you in jail myself! Tell me you're not doing this again! I swear I will kill you dead! Oh my God, what have you done?" "Aunt Bee" my foot! She confessed it all to her husband as I listened in shock. She was embezzling, and embezzling in a massive way. I was stunned. I looked at the phone as I broke out in a cold sweat. I couldn't believe what I was hearing and, moreover, couldn't believe that I was hearing it! It was such a surreal moment that I remember as if it were yesterday. Danny finally picked up, and it blocked the bleed-over. I said, "Danny, you are *not* going to believe what is going on. Please get over here as fast as you can. I'll explain when you get here." Within five minutes, he was standing in my doorway. I tried to explain what had happened, but how could I?

I ignored my instincts and gave her the **benefit of the doubt.**

I called Theresa into my office and told her I "knew." She tried to lie, but when I repeated verbatim both ends of her conversation with her husband, she folded like a pup tent in a hurricane. She confessed it all, and "all" was some kind of story. She had been embezzling money from me practically since day one. It was all premeditated. She had set me up, and despite my uneasy feelings, I'd been had. Had, big time! She was smart, as many BAITERs are. She would write out checks for all of my bills, present them to me for signature, and then stuff them in the bottom of the drawer. If the bills totaled $11,962, she would then transfer $11,962 out of the account to make it look like that money had gone out to pay bills when, in fact, it had gone to her. When past due notices came in, she intercepted them so I never had a clue. She bought cars for some of her children, made the down payment on a house for another one, and was stacking money big time—to the tune of six figures. It was a devastating "double whammy" for me and my family, because the money was gone and the bills, like my credit card, were still unpaid.

Simply put, I got conned. I got conned by a well-disguised BAITER who was running a scam and using religion, God, and family to cover it. She knew what was important to me; she pushed what she knew would resonate with my value system. I ignored my instincts and gave her the *benefit of the doubt*. I thought that was "the thing to do." And in a perfectly just world, it just might be the thing to do. But in the *real* world, where you and I actually live, it simply allowed that wolf in sheep's clothing to pull the wool right over my eyes.

Scanning Your Life

Just flip through today's newspaper or go online, and look at the top 100 news stories over the past year to see how many of them involved exactly the kind of people I'm talking about. Here's a handful of names to make my point: Bernie Madoff, who swindled investors out of billions of dollars in the biggest Ponzi scheme in history; Jared Lee Loughner, who shot Congresswoman Gabrielle Giffords and killed six people, including a federal judge and a 9-year-old girl; Jerry Sandusky, who used his foundation and his position on the coaching staff at Penn State to sexually abuse teenage and pre-teenage boys; Wade Michael Page, the white supremacist who committed suicide after killing six members of a Sikh temple in a suburb of Milwaukee; Rielle Hunter, who cheated with Sen. John Edwards and then wrote a book about their affair and went on the air criticizing *his* wife, Elizabeth Edwards, the woman she had victimized, who had just died of cancer; Levi Aron, who pleaded guilty to kidnapping and dismembering an 8-year-old boy who had been on his way home from a day camp in Brooklyn. And how about the endless string of female teachers who had sex with their underage students? I could go on and on.

I know you can make your own list, even though your BAIT-ERs, like mine, probably didn't make the headlines: your sister who loves to start trouble and cause drama, your two-faced friend who stabbed you in the back thinking you wouldn't find out, a spouse who cheated and the concubine with whom he did it, the registered sex offender down the street, the co-worker who takes credit for your work, the gossip who betrayed your trust and embarrassed you, the jealous friend who tells blatant lies about you, the service person you hire to work in your home who pretends to befriend you while all the time padding his bill and cheating you, the boss who berates you in front of others, your mother-in-law who disrespects your boundaries and doesn't seem to understand that her little boy is now 40 with his own wife (you) and three children—and needs to butt out and leave you alone! So, how do you ferret these folks out so you can keep an eye on them or eliminate them from your personal space?

I know you can make your own list, even though your BAITERs, like mine, probably didn't make the headlines.

The good news is there are some tip-offs—some patterns, traits, and characteristics that reveal who these BAITERs, these users and abusers, are. These are what psychologists call "identifiers"—things that mark these types of people like a sign on their forehead. By the time you finish this chapter, you should have a keen sense of how to identify people like this, before they get to you. This knowledge is a cornerstone of the new "Life Code."

As I described in the introduction, I came up with this list of common traits by first doing a really honest (and painful) audit of some of the BAITERs I have encountered in my personal life and then by performing an exhaustive review of the professional literature. I also spoke to some of my most trusted colleagues about their own opinions and experiences. It was really interesting how each and every person I reached out to passionately "dove in" to the analysis. They all related to the challenge because not one of them had been immune! Through this personal and professional analysis and with a lot of great help reviewing and refining the lists I had made, I compiled one list of the most observable identifiers to help you spot these BAITERs coming from a mile away—before they have a chance to do harm to you and your loved ones.

Sometimes, but not always, these BAITERs find their way to mental-health professionals, often because it's court-ordered, and so they have become the subject of much research, diagnosis, and debate. So, when relevant, I weighed all of that data as well. They have, across time, been referred to as "psychopaths," "sociopaths," "antisocial personalities," "borderline personalities," and "paranoids" among many, many others. Diagnostically it is certainly not a "one-size-fits-all" situation. But diagnosticians typically tend to try to separate distinct syndromes, not find a composite of many. My goal was exactly the opposite. For me, this is not an academic exercise; it is a real-world "applied" wisdom that I seek—a wisdom you can *use* every day. These people come in different shapes, sizes, and styles, but they *do* come, and if you are like me and everyone else I know, they are very likely already in your life as you are reading this.

To give you some insight into how the psychological and psychiatric professions deal with BAITERs, at least in part, let's use the diagnosis of the antisocial personality disorder (ASPD) as an example, remembering many other diagnoses may apply individually or in combination. The National Institutes of Mental Health (NIMH) states that antisocial personality disorder is a mental health condition in which a person has a long-term pattern of manipulating, exploiting, or violating the rights of others. The condition is common in people in prison.

In the fourth edition of the American Psychiatric Association's *Diagnostic and Statistical Manual*, this disorder is characterized by "a pervasive pattern of disregard for, and violation of, the rights of others that begins in childhood or early adolescence and continues into adulthood."

They can get you in trouble just by your being in the wrong place at the wrong time.

Those diagnosed with ASPD as adults were commonly diagnosed with "conduct disorder" as children. Fire-setting and cruelty to animals during childhood are linked to the development of antisocial personality disorder.

According to the NIMH, the causes of antisocial personality disorder are unknown. Genetic factors and child abuse are believed to contribute to the development of this condition. People with an antisocial or alcoholic parent are at increased risk. Far more men than women are affected. The effectiveness of treatment for antisocial personality disorder is not known. Treatments that show the person the negative consequences of illegal behavior seem to hold the most promise.

From your own experience, you probably know people who routinely behave as if the rules of society simply don't apply to them. It's absolutely imperative that you develop an urgent awareness of who these people are because they are dangerous to be around. They can get you in trouble just by your being in the wrong place at the wrong time. Even worse, the rules they break can be in their interactions with you because you become an unwitting target. I want you to join me in performing what I call a "life scan." This is an intuitive-based "risk assessment" to start you down the road of listening to and trusting your instincts.

Exercise: I want you, using the following table, to write down the different categories in which you interact with other people. This may include categories such as work, social, family, sports, hobbies, religion, romantic, and even online. Then I want you to make a list of the people you routinely encounter in each of those categories. In just a few paragraphs from now, I'm going to begin to give you some very specific and observable identifiers that tend to make any of these people who might be dangerous much more obvious. But before we get to that, what I would like for you to do is tune in to your instincts: What does your *gut* tell you about each of the people you put on your list? You can categorize them as "safe," "neutral," "suspicious," or "dangerous." You may need to create more sheets if you know a lot of people because I want you to be thorough.

Remember, all I'm asking for right now is your instinct. Don't worry about being wrong at this point. Be honest with yourself, even if it feels like you are being harsh, because no one will see this work except you. Once you have some identifiers and some more information, you may change your opinion in either direction about anybody on your list. But right now, I just want you to acknowledge your gut-level reaction. I think when you start listening to your gut, you'll find some people who end up on your "suspicious" or "dangerous" list are people you've always

WARNING BELLS

Think of all the people in your current life who give you that "funny feeling," that nagging sense that something isn't quite right. List the area of your life in which you interact with them, include their names, and then describe the feeling they give you. Remember, this is for your eyes only, so be honest with yourself.

AREA OF LIFE	NAME OF PERSON	GUT FEELING

had funny feelings about but you just didn't know why. I think you're going to be saying, "Wow, I really do have a strange feeling about this person; I just never acknowledged it because I didn't want to seem negative or judgmental, and I couldn't quite put my finger on why. But now that I'm specifically approaching it with a purpose in mind, I can see that I've been ignoring these feelings for a long time." Give yourself permission to acknowledge your

feelings even if you can't defend or articulate them, let a
any proof. By the way, if you feel that way about certain
hope you're wrong. I hope when you do your homework,
out it was something completely benign that was causing your
unease. But if not, I want them to go on your watch list.

I don't want you to have to say later, "If I only knew *then* what
I know *now*." You can "know it now," and you can clean up your
life and get real about people who might pose a threat. Like we
say about physical disease, "Early detection and early intervention can be outcome-determinative." And don't forget, "An
ounce of prevention is worth a pound of cure." It all fits!

> *I don't want you to have to say later, "If I only knew*
> **then** *what I know* now."

How do you start? You've made your "gut-check" list, so now
let's put some science to it. You need to learn the identifiers of
the people we're talking about—the BAITERs who lie, cheat, and
steal, and worse, without any regard for anyone else.

The "Evil Eight" Identifiers of the BAITER

#1: They see the world through a lens of arrogant entitlement and frequently treat people as targets.

This one is hard for most people to grasp. People tell me all the
time: "I hear your words, but I just don't *get* it." But you have to
understand that the BAITERs don't live in the same world you
do. Their world is defined solely by their own needs and desires.
Other people, and other people's needs and desires, just aren't
real to them. You might approach a situation simply to enjoy it,

learn from it, or just do it for the sake of doing it. The BAITER is always "on the make" looking for a way to capitalize. A lot of these people are so crooked they have to screw their socks on in the morning! They can't *not* victimize people if they see an opening. They will lie when the truth would do better because it is just their nature.

And by the way, they're not going to feel any worse about it than they would crossing the street. Those are nonemotional events to them. If they find an angle to "get ahead," they will do it and do it right over the top of you. If they can cheat you or hurt you or your loved ones to gain some advantage, they will—without a blink. The goal is getting the advantage, not nurturing some relationship with you.

If they find an angle to "get ahead," they will do it and do it right over the top of you.

You might inadvertently invite a BAITER to your home for dinner or drinks. Innocent enough, right? Maybe, but he might also be thinking about how he can "use" this access to your home to his advantage. If you are his boss, he may be thinking how he can drop comments around co-workers about being invited to your home. It is power to him, so how can he use it? If it is a "friend," she may be looking for flaws that she can gossip about to other "friends" to cause you embarrassment and, by comparison, make herself look better. Or maybe he is thinking how he can criticize you to others concerning your house: "You would *not* believe how much booze she has in there!" "They have a nice room, but their children are so mistreated and abused and crammed into a hole in the basement. They're so selfish!"

Maybe your houseguest was that woman your husband *worked* with. She wanted to take something from you, something that was yours—your husband. Think back: Maybe months before you found out what was going on, she was at your house, chatting pleasantly with you but all the while thinking: "She has no idea what's going on between her husband and me. I could get him to leave her with a snap of my fingers, and it would be her fault for not paying attention to him." And do you remember? She was smiling all the while.

If a home-wrecker wants your husband, to her,
you're *the problem she has to overcome.*

To protect yourself from these people, you have to understand their motivations and think like they do, but never think they are not plotting at your expense or at least scanning for an opening. It's simply who they are; it is as natural to them as brushing your teeth is to you. My uncle was a career policeman, and he always said locks are for honest people. An honest person walks up to a locked door and sees a barrier—obviously whoever owns this property doesn't want me on the other side of it. But a crook sees a locked door as an obstacle, merely something to overcome.

If a BAITER is hired at your workplace and you have the job he actually wants, that's just a locked door to him. You're just an obstacle to get past. If a home-wrecker wants your husband, to her, *you're* the problem she has to overcome. Your marriage means nothing to her.

These people have a sense of entitlement about everything, no matter what it is or who possesses it. Their attitude is, "This is mine; you just have it currently." They think, "I'd like that," and their mental tumblers churn: "Now, how can I get it?" If the BAITER wants your job, your house, your husband, or your life, you better hunker down because you've got a fight on your hands. My goal is to prepare you so that the BAITER does not have the element of surprise and can't launch a sneak attack.

#2: They lack empathy.

As I look around my house, if I don't like something—say this candle on my coffee table—I can just throw it away. I'm not going to feel bad about it; I don't think, "Oh, I've treated my wax so poorly." I'm not going to have an emotional reaction or worry about hurt feelings, because candles don't have feelings.

That's how BAITERs think about *people*! They're cold. It's not that they don't share your feelings, which is what sympathy is all about. They don't have any regard for, or understand, your feelings—or human feelings in general—in the first place, which is what empathy is all about. It never occurs to them how you might be hurting or suffering because of what they did.

It never occurs to them how you might be hurting or suffering because of what they did.

These BAITERs will betray this deficiency if they are taken beyond a "scripted" response. They may know how to mimic empathy, repeating what they have heard others say or what some therapist may have told them empathetic people say. But once they use up the buzzwords or sound bites, they are out of their depth and may seem really inept or cold. Additionally, you will see them do some things that indicate they don't appreciate a point of view other than their own. They may have a history of cruelty to animals (which you may not know about but might be able to find out), or you may see them behave coldly and unconcernedly—if, for example, you are driving together and see a puppy in traffic or hear a story about an animal being hurt or injured. Beyond a script, they will show you a callousness, without even being aware they've tipped you off. Listen and watch, and they will out themselves to you soon enough.

#3: They are incapable of feeling remorse/guilt and don't learn from situation to situation.

How can they do the things they do? Because they pursue pure gratification without fear of consequence or without the burden of conscience. They do not have the ability to feel guilt or sorrow. They do not have the capacity to feel bad about what they have done. Think about that; if they never get a signal from their brain that says "Stop!" then why would they ever do so? Someone who lacks empathy, has no conscience, and feels no remorse also lacks an understanding of normal human cause and effect. Those home invaders who murdered that family saw the situation strictly from their own, selfish point of view. The only thing that even sort of registered with them was what was in it for them. After killing the parents, it made perfect sense *to them* to kill that 12-year-old boy. After all, he saw them kill his mother and father, and they had to get rid of witnesses so they'd never get caught. (Of course, they did get caught anyway, as BAITERs often do.) In fact, to this way of thinking, there could not have been any other outcome. From their perspective, there was no upside to letting him live and no downside to killing him. How could the killers reach any other conclusion? Of course they killed him; the fact that they did so by drowning him in scalding hot water was beside the point. They just didn't care. Extreme example? Yes, but even if the stakes change, the dynamic is the same.

It's not just cold-blooded killers who behave like this. Remember that home-wrecker who was your dinner guest? She stood there smiling and talking to you while drinking a cocktail you mixed, in *your* home, all the while knowing an hour earlier she was having sex with *your* husband at a hotel.

They can appear to be witty and charming, but it's all subterfuge.

She could act that way only because she has no regard for or insight into how her behavior is compromising her character or how she is trespassing into *your* life. Not only does she lack empathy, but her conscience is turned off. She simply doesn't have the moral concerns the rest of us have. These BAITERs act without any of the barriers, any of the boundaries, any of the concerns that we would have, and that's why we have such a hard time understanding how they can *do* the things they do.

They can appear to be witty and charming, but it's all subterfuge. They are not interested in you as a person; they have a hidden agenda and no feelings about it at all.

Someone whose conscience is turned off is capable of almost anything.

Where they go wrong

Notice I say "almost anything." In the end, there are real-world limits to what these people can do, because they're flawed human beings. Most of all, they lack insight—the ability to learn from their mistakes. They don't even think they make mistakes, because if they are caught and confronted, it's always someone else's fault. This flaw can be really, really helpful in spotting them because they can't recognize when their story, excuse, or explanation is not "playing well" in the room. They might be advancing a really transparent lie, and they have no ability to see that you aren't buying it because they don't know how to consider your point of view. The lack of empathy and lack of ability to feel remorse are big tip-offs.

This lack of insight is a big reason why BAITERs are so resistant to psychological therapy. They rarely seek treatment on their own. They may start therapy only when required to by a court. And then they often don't have the self-awareness to benefit from counseling. They are so narcissistic that they can't get outside of themselves to see what they are doing or what they caused. They simply can't conceive of a real alternative to their way of doing things. So, they're locked into behavioral patterns and make the same mistakes over and over again.

#4: They are irresponsible, self-destructive, and disregard the well-being of others.

This may seem paradoxical at first. If these BAITERs are so self centered, how can they *also* be self-destructive? The answer is precisely because they have an unreal sense of their own power. They also do not register consequences. To them, everyone else is a fool, but they never are themselves. So if they do something reckless and get hurt themselves, they don't learn not to do it again because, after all, it just couldn't have been their fault!

These BAITERs tend to seem accident-prone, but it is really just that they don't follow the rules. They ignore weather reports, drive at unsafe speeds in the rain, and then crash their cars—all because they don't think the rules of the road apply to them. They are often substance abusers, and some researchers believe they need to take risks in order to feel alive and aroused. They take risks that we wouldn't because their narcissism makes them irresponsible. They think they are "bulletproof."

They don't just deceive other people; they deceive themselves into thinking that they're special—that they're not subject to normal cause and effect. They don't believe the rules apply to them.

#5: They thrive on drama and crisis.

Their unhealthy behavior often begins to show sometime around puberty. Before adolescence, it seems all children are self-centered, but most gradually become socialized. Normal children learn that other people have rights, that they can't always get what they want, and that they have to get along to get ahead. BAITERs love conflict and controversy; it accompanies them seemingly at every turn. They need the drama to feel alive, so they create it. They stir things up and love to see everyone getting upset. Drama and crisis are currency to them because they love the power to make people react. They thrive on a good fight, a good scandal, a good drama.

Most children learn the difference between assertiveness and aggressiveness. They're brought up by their parents to understand that it's okay to assert their own rights, but it's *not* okay to be aggressive and trample on other people's rights.

Drama and crisis are currency to them because they love the power to make people react. They thrive on a good fight, a good scandal, a good drama.

BAITERs never learn these lessons. Instead, they start acting out when they can't get their way. As I said, boys are cruel to animals, start fires, and get into fistfights. The BAITER girls start dressing provocatively, using foul language, and engaging in sexual promiscuity at an early age.

They are often *very* angry and arrogant, which shows just below the surface. Over time, their lack of impulse control and inability to relate to other people as human beings keep landing them in hot water. They have a low tolerance for frustration, a low threshold for engaging in aggression, and poor impulse control. This leads them into frequent conflicts with authority figures (teachers, law enforcement, supervisors at work).

But for every time BAITERs get caught, they get away with their behavior much more often. The worst of them may wind up in juvenile detention and then jail or prison, but most of them seem to stay one step ahead of disaster and often escape any serious accountability. That means they are living in your world and readily able to mess with you!

> *But for every time BAITERs get caught, they get away with their behavior much more often.*

#6: They brag about outsmarting other people.

BAITERs are braggarts, and if you pay attention, they will show you who they are. They actually brag about doing something that you and any halfway moral person would regard as cheating. But to them, it's not being dishonest—it's just being smarter than, and one step ahead of, the other guy, some sucker who got what he deserved.

"I was just smarter than he was. I mean, we had this deal, and we were partners. But I knew what I was doing, and he didn't, so I wound up with all the assets while he got all the debt. Now he's bankrupt, and I'm way ahead."

He's bragging about screwing his partner over, but he doesn't see it like that. As I said, with no insight, BAITERs never know how what they're saying is playing in the room. They're so narcissistic, they think everybody will see things from their point of view. They say things like, "That guy is so trusting, he'll be easy pickings," or "She's so asleep at the switch, she'll never even see me coming 'til I'm gone." "You snooze, you lose." The fact that you are aghast and can't believe what you're hearing is lost on them.

#7: They have a pattern of short-term relationships.

They can't sustain a relationship because they're hollow inside. They have nothing to give—although they can give the illusion of giving, even over-giving, to make you feel indebted. It's nothing but a way to aggrandize themselves, however. Eventually people get what they give, and BAITERs don't give enough, or anything at all, so whatever relationships they begin can't last. They are incapable of making authentic human connections. You won't have to ask many questions to tease this out of them because their favorite topic is themselves. As long as you will listen, they will spew it out.

#8: They live in a fantasy world marked by delusion.

When it comes to how they see themselves, BAITERs are nothing short of delusional. They may see themselves as victims or in some exalted status but always in a manner that justifies and motivates their self-serving agenda. They are like "method actors" who live the delusion as though it were reality. They can almost be so convinced of and immersed in the fantasy that they could "straight line" a polygraph. Amateur liars will, when challenged, become nervous and ill at ease; BAITERs, on the other hand, are pros. And the delusions typically extend to others. For example, they may construct a fantasy in which you are the exploiter and are contemptible for being who you are and having what you have. Within their delusional system, they are entitled, and they will take, use, and abuse in a reckless and wanton fashion. Delusions of grandeur cause them to condescend to you with a contempt they may attempt to hide but always feel. These people are mean and cold, and you are just a target. If their delusions turn to those of persecution, they can become urgently dangerous in the name of self-preservation.

Paranoia makes it difficult, if not impossible, to sustain human relationships. In journalistic descriptions of serial killers, paranoid people are looking for ways to harm or manipulate other people. In truth, those suffering from paranoia are afraid of other people and turn to aggression to defend themselves. They assume other people are out to get them, and they act out of a distorted sense of self-defense.

So, there you have the "Evil Eight." Specialized knowledge and awareness are key components of the new "Life Code," and these eight identifiers are critical information. Now that you have it, a level of vigilance will yield a very different perspective than before.

Paranoia makes it difficult, if not impossible, to sustain human relationships.

Benefit of the Doubt: Why?

By now, your instincts should be telling you there are people out there, and probably in your life, who are just not okay. I don't want you to panic, and I don't want you to become a cynic, but I do want you to listen to that inner voice—a voice that may give you the sense of unease that security specialist Gavin de Becker calls "the gift of fear." If you feel that, you must ask yourself what's bothering you. When you do, think about everything in this chapter. Go back through the "Evil Eight," and see what applies. If you're still not sure, ask somebody you trust if the criteria really apply to the person in question, from their point of view.

What you should do is suspend judgment until you know more.

Whatever you do, don't ignore that feeling. I know that goes against how you think you should behave. We're taught not to be suspicious. We don't want to be paranoid. We've been told since childhood that we should give people the benefit of the doubt, that we should trust people.

But what I'm saying is you should trust yourself *first*. In the end, that's the only way you can protect yourself and your family. That doesn't mean you should be suspicious of everyone, any more than you should trust everyone. What you should do is suspend judgment until you know more. To do otherwise is to discard data and ignore the available information. That never makes sense.

We have all been taught to give people the *benefit of the doubt*, as though doing so is a virtue, as though it is a reflection of our evolved character, the moral high ground. The new "Life Code" calls for a very different attitude and practice. I think it is reckless, not virtuous, to blindly give people the benefit of the doubt. I'm an incurable optimist, I really am, but I don't give people the benefit of the doubt. I just don't. Nor do I automatically judge them negatively. I approach people from a neutral standpoint, then start gathering data from the first impression on, and finally form an opinion when I have enough information. I don't judge books by their covers, so to speak, and neither should you. I want you to rethink your first instinct of trusting people until they prove unworthy. I want you to say, "You know what? I'm not going to do that anymore, nor am I going to prejudge somebody as bad. I'm going to keep an open mind and gather data. But if my instincts are telling me there is something not quite right with someone, I am going to listen to *me*, and they're going to go on my special watch list."

And by the way, you don't have to let everyone into your life in the same way. You can have differing levels of trust, appropriate to your level of involvement with people—strangers, casual acquaintances, people you deal with in business, neighbors, close friends, family members.

One of my dearest friends is a brilliant billionaire. I could call him right now and say, "Hey, I need you here; I need your help." And I don't care what he was doing—he would stop everything, call his pilot, fire up the burner, and be on my doorstep as fast as his private jet could get him here. But, he's a notorious womanizer. So, if I had a daughter in college or young sister, I definitely wouldn't say, "Oh, by the way, could you please stop in Dallas on the way and pick her up?" I would trust him with my life but not with my women! Ha! I'm kidding, sort of.

There are other people I wouldn't do business with, but I might not tell them to get out of my life. I wouldn't have them in my home, I wouldn't lend them my car, and I certainly wouldn't entrust my kids to them. But if they're going be at the Sunday social, am I going to skip it? Nope. I don't think they're going to pick my pocket, but that doesn't mean I'm going to invite them in where they could hurt me or take advantage of me. Maybe you have neighbors you say hello to but wouldn't invite into your home. That's not being inhospitable; that's being careful and recognizing limits and boundaries. I have "tennis buddies" who I have "known" for years and trust 100 percent at the *level of my involvement* with them. I trust them to reliably show up when we set up a game, to not cheat, to not pout, and to not go nuts if they have a bad day. I trust them to play hard, compete well, and generally be pleasant to spend two hours with. Before I would take the relationship to the next level, I would need more information. That they are a good "tennis buddy" is a positive, but it does not mean they would be a good business partner. Plato said, "You can learn more about a man in an hour of play than in a year of conversation," so it does help—it is data, but it is not sufficient.

> *I think it is reckless, not virtuous, to blindly give people the benefit of the doubt.*

What do you need to take a relationship to the next level? Relevant observations and information from which you can make attributions to the person. If it is to determine whether a business relationship is prudent, you need references from people who have been where you are thinking of going. You need a credit and legal history. You need to pay attention to the relevant values they espouse. Given hypotheticals, how do they problem solve? *Do not* assume that because they are fun to fish with, or go to the movies with, that they are worthy of betting any part of your family's future on. *No benefit of the doubt.* That is just bad life management and is excluded from the new "Life Code."

Remember I said at the beginning of the chapter that there were people in your past about whom you'd say, "I wish I knew then what I know now?" Well, if you've been paying attention to this chapter, you may never have to say that again.

When Warning Bells Go Off

Now, before I wrap up this chapter, there is one other scan I want you to do. I recommend you get into the habit of doing what I call a "situational scan." Before I even tell you what I mean, let me assure you that I'm not trying to turn you into a Navy Seal or James Bond or some freaky paranoid who walks into a room and gets all shifty-eyed. But I do want you to develop that "urgent awareness" I have been talking about.

For some reason, I have had a particular habit throughout my life, even before I was trained in the field of psychology. That habit was to come into any new situation or setting and immediately, consciously, and systematically "scan" the room to get a feel for what was going on and who was involved. I believe it is a good and healthy thing to have social sensitivity. Most people have social sensitivity to some degree. We "read" our audience. Are they bored and wanting to change the subject or move on? Are they confused and frustrated? Are they loving what you are doing and offering you encouragement, verbal or nonverbal, to carry on? Tuning into this "vibe" is social sensitivity. I want you to consciously and purposefully take that social sensitivity to the next level.

If Robin and I go to a restaurant, I've always had the habit of trying to position myself where I could see the largest part of the room. (In Texas we call that the gunfighter's chair! It would drive me crazy to have my back exposed to the entire room.) Once seated, if not before, I immediately, discreetly, but purposefully do a visual scan of the room. If the guy three tables away is getting drunk and noisy, I don't do anything about it, but I do make a mental note. If a couple sitting next to us is arguing and the man is shaking his finger in the woman's face, I just take that into account. If there is a table full of fans with University of Oklahoma clothing and paraphernalia on and they're next to a table with University of Texas clothing and paraphernalia, I add that to my mental checklist. If things "get drunk out," this could become a volatile situation. If, sometime during the evening, trouble erupts in any of these noted areas, I'm not saying I'll get involved, but I also won't be blindsided. I won't be caught unawares.

Most people have social sensitivity to some degree. We "read" our audience.

If, on a more personal note, some guy is really flirting with my wife, even a little bit, I pay attention. Robin is very good at handling this sort of thing on her own and probably doesn't need my help in the least. But if she does, I'm not going to spend the first five minutes getting "caught up" on what she's talking about.

If someone, just out of the blue, becomes uncharacteristically and totally enchanted with you, charmed by you, and focused on you, that might feel good, but come on—at least ask yourself, "why?" Maybe you just woke up today and have a newfound magnetism, but then again maybe not.

If someone is staring at you, pay attention. Watch for agitation, animated behavior, bizarre behavior, or emotionally charged conversation or interactions. Be ultra-aware if it is a situation where alcohol is being consumed, because it could be a factor.

I was recently attending my good friend Ron White's comedy show at one of the casinos in Las Vegas. After the show (hilarious by the way, a "must" on your bucket list), a group of us— including Robin; Ron and his fiancée, Margot; and my son, Jay, and our daughter-in-law, Erica—had dinner at a restaurant in the casino. When we were done, I called for security to escort us through the casino, but they were given the wrong instructions on where to meet us. After waiting a bit, we decided to go on without them. Bad idea. Poor situational awareness. I knew better but hoped that if I kept my feet moving and got to the elevators, we would be okay. Wrong.

If someone, just out of the blue, becomes uncharacteristically and totally enchanted with you, charmed by you, and focused on you, that might feel good, but come on—at least ask yourself, "why?"

Now, please understand, I don't consider myself some big celebrity who needs bodyguards and escorts, but I have to say, late hours plus free alcohol plus a vacation mentality of relaxed standards plus opportunity add up to trouble every time. I think maybe because I have been on television every day for ten years, people feel some degree of familiarity, which the vast majority of the time is just wonderful, but add in all the other factors I mentioned, and that dynamic can change in a hurry.

I've been in casinos late at night before. By the time it's 2 or 3 a.m., a lot of patrons are beyond drunk. Invariably, some guy, or three or four, who have had a big bowl of that "loudmouth soup," decide they want to have a session with Dr. Phil. And sure enough, that is exactly what happened that night. A group of highly inebriated guys from Atlanta saw me and started yelling and running over.

"Hey, Dr. Phil, how's that working for you?" (Very original!)

"Hey, my wife quotes you all the f---ing time!"

"Hey, you have to come up to my room and say hi to my wife; she won't believe this s---! She said you said I was a moron!"

"My b----- wife watched your show every day, and she said she saw no future and left me cold after eight years." He says all of this while burping and spraying spit all over my shirt. "Why do you think she did that?" (I, of course, am thinking but not saying, "I can't imagine why she would not be just plum giddy with a guy as charming as you!")

Okay, now you can guess how this went down when I declined to perform group therapy on drunks or go awaken some total stranger from a deep sleep with her drunken, loudmouth husband. He wasn't happy, and neither was the man their drunk friend crashed into while trying to get over to talk to me. Fortunately, security did show up and avert an even more awkward situation.

It is just good practice to do a situational scan and have situational awareness when you are out in the world. I'm sure you already do this to some degree. If you and your husband and children walk into a roadside café and it's full of 50 or so Hell's Angels roughhousing and being unruly, I'm guessing your alarm bells would go off. If you were in a dark alley walking to your car and you heard several men coming up behind you with rapid footsteps, again, bells would go off. So, you do have the capability. I just want to lower the threshold at which those bells sound.

I can best summarize the "Evil Eight" by describing the last BAITER who tried to "put the britches" on Robin and me.

It is just good practice to do a situational scan and have situational awareness when you are out in the world.

Dr. Chase (name changed, but all other facts, though summarized, are very real) arranged a social meeting with us through an acquaintance. Within the first ten minutes he was name-dropping like he was calling roll on a red carpet. He knew Robin had written two #1 *New York Times* best sellers dealing with women's health and well-being and is a highly sought-after speaker and television guest. The good doctor was so arrogant that it was obvious he believed that, just because he was offering, she should: a) become his patient and unqualifiedly endorse him; b) arrange for him to be on my show and our son's show *The Doctors*; c) overlook his constant drama, criticism, and conflict with colleagues and his third wife; and d) coauthor a book with him, with his name of course being the first, because he is, after all, a doctor. Dr. Chase was so narcissistic, he truly believed that he was destined to be famous and that Robin should be grateful for the chance to ride on his train to the promised land. How did he fare on our instinct meter and score on our "Evil Eight" checklist?

The instinct meter was pinging, and we listened to *us*. This guy was way too "slick." He drove a Bentley and made sure we knew it. We also knew he had filed bankruptcy within the last three months. He touted three failed marriages and a hostile, pouty girlfriend with whom he bickered and disrespected. He clearly had a sense of entitlement (#1). He had no sensitivity to the awkwardness of his aggressive "pitch" at a social function (#2 and #3). Repeated conflict with colleagues, being ostracized for his unprofessional conduct (#4). Constant drama, personally and professionally (#5). Publicly belittling others to aggrandize himself (#6) and multiple failed relationships (#7). And if he thought either Robin or I would ever get involved with him, he was definitely delusional (#8). He was batting a thousand. By the way, he was confused and appalled when he was told we had no interest in any shared projects or in having him on either of our shows! Add us to the list of failed and *very* short-term relationships! A definite BAITER.

3

The "Bad Guys"/ "BAITER" Secret Playbook

"Don't be afraid of enemies who attack you. Be afraid of the friends who flatter you."

—Dale Carnegie

If BAITERs lead such dysfunctional lives, how do they manage to succeed? How can they take advantage of the rest of us with such apparent ease? How does that scheming home-wrecker steal your husband? How does that con man swindle you out of your money? Why does that brown-nosing, sycophant suck-up, backstabber get the promotion you deserve? How do they get next to you, worm their way into your confidence, gain information, and then use it to betray you? How does the abusive husband get his wife to stay with him despite his cruel and demeaning treatment of her? How *do* molesters find and get close to vulnerable families and children?

In the previous chapter, you learned how to identify a BAITER (Backstabbers, Abusers, Imposters, Takers, Exploiters, Reckless) and how to do a "life scan" and a "situation scan" to determine potential threats in your life and the lives of your loved ones. You discovered how to spot those in your life who are potential threats by "grading their paper" against the "Evil Eight" identifiers.

1. **Do they see the world through a lens of arrogant entitlement and frequently treat people as targets?**

2. **Do they lack empathy?**

3. **Are they incapable of feeling remorse/guilt and fail to learn from situation to situation?**

4. **Are they irresponsible and self-destructive, and do they disregard the well-being of others?**

5. **Do they thrive on drama and crisis?**

6. **Do they brag about outsmarting other people?**

7. **Do they have a pattern of short-term relationships?**

8. **Do they live in a fantasy world, marked by delusion?**

In addition to learning to "listen" to your instincts, you are now equipped with "BAITER Radar," sensitized to these identifiers that make these dangerous people much easier to detect in your life before they can sink their fangs into you. Simply by doing some homework, either you can gather enough history to "out" them or you can make important attributions about and to them, based on observations of behaviors that you are now trained to recognize in real time.

Even though you're now armed with a checklist, you must guard against being in denial or being lulled to sleep. I have spoken about an "urgent awareness" because it is beyond likely that these BAITERs are already in your life right now, maybe as close as the person sitting next to you on your couch. Remember, in the new "Life Code" that I am proposing, giving the "benefit of the doubt" is an outdated, obsolete, and naïve concept that can be extremely dangerous. Once again, I am *not* asking you to become cynical or highhandedly judgmental. But I *am* asking you to attend to factual, observable information to determine the required level of self-protection, which can range from paying extra-close attention to someone all the way to lacing up your running shoes and heading for the hills (or anywhere, as long as it's far away from the toxic and dangerous individual).

And, by the way, subtlety in these endeavors is not always your friend. Sometimes you will encounter people who are "on the bubble" as to whether they are going to exploit you. You don't want to tempt someone by projecting yourself as such an inattentive, easy target that they just can't help take the shot. There is a reason that banks, stores, and casinos have "uniformed" security officers who watch not just the customers but also the employees. An overt show of force, an obvious layer of security, will deter a large percentage of potential bad guys.

My dad used to say, "You put a fox in the hen house, and he will have chicken for dinner every single night." He was right, and so am I when I tell you that if you don't watch the people in your life as they deal with your money, your family, your reputation, or even your mate, you are at a much higher risk of being exploited than if you maintain an *obvious* level of vigilance. In short, watch the people in your life, and let them know they are being watched. This is not about being paranoid; it is about being vigilant and urgently aware. And the less you know about those you are watching, the closer you need to watch. Is this a sad state of affairs? Maybe, but it is what it is, and pretending it isn't only makes it worse.

So, now you know that you need to spot them, and you have the tools to do so. But, now you need to do more than just spot them; I want you to understand *how* they think and *how* they take advantage of you and your loved ones. It's time to get inside their heads to unlock and master their secret "playbook." This is the playbook that jumped off my office wall after looking at all the BAITERs in my life and slapped me right in the face—bam! I already knew that they lied, cheated, and stole. What I hadn't articulated to myself or anyone else is *how* they actually did it and got away with it.

In the BAITERs I'm describing, we're talking about a breed of exploiter that can be complex and multilayered, so I want you to learn their specific tricks, tools, and tactics. You've got to not only see them but know how to neutralize them so they will decide they are better off moving on. They do that because, all of a sudden, you're just way too much trouble to put one over on. You need to understand their playbook—their strategic plan, their tactical manual. I get that poking around "inside their head," while very interesting, can be very unsettling.

As a clinical psychologist, a courtroom consultant, an author of books on human behavior, and the host of the show focused on human functioning, I've spent decades dealing with BAITERs and their victims, and I know as well as anyone what's involved in truly becoming familiar with these people. To predict their behavior, you have to see the world through their eyes and let your mind take a walk on the dark side. You need to have the same dialogue they have with themselves. You have to be able to switch gears and think like *they* do.

So, let's open up the BAITERs' secret "playbook." And let me be very clear about why. Think about this analogy: A father has a precious daughter who has reached her teenage years and is ready to start dating. Now Dad, having himself once been a hairy-legged teenage boy fueled by pure testosterone, has some insight into how these young men think. So, he wants to be his daughter's "friend at the factory" and tell her all of the tricks and traps that a horny, young teenage boy may use to, well…get next to her.

To predict their behavior, you have to see the world through their eyes and let your mind take a walk on the dark side.

If Dad tells her every "pick-up line" and every strategy or angle a boy is likely to use to compromise her, she is way ahead of the game. If Dad tells her that a boy is likely to say, for example, "If you loved me, you would," and then some dude, in fact, uses that lame line, bells are going to go off like crazy in her head. She'll be thinking, "Wow, this guy is as predictable as an old plow horse! He better come at me with more game than that, because I've got his playbook." But if nobody ever bothered to sit her down and let her know what they're going to come at her with, she would be much more vulnerable than she is once her dad briefs her.

The same is true for you. This is *our* "sit-down," and I want to tell you what the BAITERs are going to come at you with. My hope is that, like the father's daughter, when it happens to you—and it will—you will say, "Wow, this is exactly what Dr. Phil and I talked about. They're doing exactly what he said they would. They're going to need a lot more game than that to get to me, because I have an urgent awareness and I value myself too much to be used and exploited." Dad was trying to keep them out of his innocent daughter's pants. I'm trying to keep them out of your pockets, your home, and maybe your pants too!

The "Nefarious 15"

So, here are what I call the "Nefarious 15." They are the 15 most nefarious "tactics," behaviors, or strategies BAITERs will use to "get to you," hurt you, and take what is yours.

#1: They infiltrate your life, seducing with promises and flattery.

I'm going to start you off with a challenge here because sometimes it's difficult to distinguish between someone who genuinely is a friend and has an interest in you and your life and someone who is trying to ingratiate and enmesh himself into your life with an ulterior motive. If, for example, we're talking about child molesters, who are certainly a subset of BAITERs, they are masters at "grooming" not only their child victim, but the victim's family. I once dealt with a tragically perfect example. Karen, a single mother in her late 20s, had a 9-year-old boy who, for the purposes of this book, I will call Jeffrey. Karen worked two jobs in an effort to provide for herself and her son. She was extremely anguished over the fact that she didn't have more time to spend with Jeffrey and that he had no male role model in his life. The hours between his dismissal from school and her arrival home at about 7 p.m. were a particular challenge.

Her neighbor, Don, was a 40-something man who lived across the street. Don was *supposedly* divorced with no children and was eager to volunteer to do things with Jeffrey. After some time of "building a relationship" with Karen and Jeffrey (actually grooming them), he told her it was crazy for her to be paying a babysitter for those after-school hours (he identified the "need") because he got home from work about the time Jeffrey would arrive from school. "Let me help out here. I think the world of

Jeffrey, and I'm happy to look after him, take him to the park, drive him to baseball practice, or whatever he might be interested in. I'm happy to do it, and it would save you money, give him a male role model, let you take a deep breath, and not worry so much about him being okay. I want to—it would be a gift to me" (and there's the "solution").

Of course, as you can imagine, such a kind offer, which fit so well into what was needed, seemed to Karen like an answer to a prayer. It was several months later that Jeffrey began to show signs of withdrawing. He became uncharacteristically sullen and moody. He began to come up with excuses not to see Don. To make a long story short, Don had infiltrated his way into their lives by building a relationship. He "understood" Karen and her challenges, he empathized with her as a mother, and he wanted to "help." He identified a *need* and then provided a *solution*. This gave him access, and he began grooming Jeffrey. First he expressed an interest in what Jeffrey was into (music, sports), and then it was horse-play, wrestling, tickling, and playing. Then it was porn movies just playing in the background, and then it escalated to the unthinkable, and this innocent boy was serially molested and ultimately raped. This sick, perverted BAITER came at mother and son with a mask of sincerity and an offer to help. He didn't snatch him off the street; he got himself invited into their lives and home.

In this example of terrible perversion, the BAITER's target is an innocent child, but even more often, the target is you and your money, reputation, job, spouse, or social position. Whether the BAITER's personal poison is perversion or greed, he (or she) must be identified and defended against when he attempts to work his way into your world. The BAITER grooms you just like they do a child, which is why you must lose your childlike trust in favor of making data-based attributions to the people in your world.

In addition to recognizing *needs* and weaknesses and providing seeming *solutions*, another infiltration tactic is the BAITERs' use of flattery. These people are basically "con artists." They instill confidence by appealing to your ego and your innate need for approval. You're going to shake your head over what I am about to tell you, but this is a powerful insight not many people have because it isn't talked about much. Research has shown a very strong connection between who we choose to believe/trust and the level of acceptance we feel from that person. Here's the deal (part of which is obvious and part of which is not): We tend to believe people who we like. And here's the key part: We tend to like those who like us. So, by extension, if someone wants to gain your trust and be believed by you, one of their most powerful tools is to make you feel liked by them. So, by further extension, if someone is trying to get you to buy into their agenda, they can advance their cause and gain more and more access and information, all just by "loving you up!" They will flatter you, laugh at your jokes, agree with your positions, support your efforts, and on and on, right up until they strike.

They instill confidence by appealing to your ego and your innate need for approval.

In Hollywood, I am especially attuned to this because it seems to be the "capital city" for flattery and insincere declarations by dysfunctional sycophants looking to get ahead. There are some good, warm, and genuine people in what has now become my world, but we do appear to have more than our share of BAITERs.

And Hollywood certainly doesn't have a monopoly on this sick system of self-destruction because you'll find it in the NBA and the NFL and anywhere there is a hierarchy. If all you are ever hearing is what you want to hear, be afraid. Be very afraid.

When someone tells you your outfit looks nice or your haircut is flattering, it's sometimes hard to know whether they're being sincere. But you will develop "measuring sticks" that work for you by listening to your instincts. For example, I'm always cautious of people who enthusiastically say, "Oh, you are sooo funny!" or "That is sooo funny!" but without actually laughing. If it was sooo funny, why aren't they sooo laughing? And if they're not sincere, if they are "working you," it behooves you to figure out why. Trust me; they aren't putting all that energy into you for no reason. They are setting you up for something, and whatever it is, it won't be a gift to you.

BAITERs do this because it works, not because it doesn't. One complaint I constantly hear from people with office jobs is that someone they work with has the ear of their boss and is always "working it." "Oh, she is such a suck-up, but it's so transparent. The boss *has* to see through her like a picture window." But based on the research I just shared, you know that, in fact, it may be working—big time. Maybe the boss *is* susceptible to her flattery. People's favorite topic in the whole wide world is, take a guess, wait for it...themselves! They want to talk about themselves more than they want to talk about you or anything else. They want to talk about their attitudes, their opinions, their beliefs, their experiences. They are like opera stars warming up for the big performance: "Me, me, me, me, me!"

So, the manipulative trifecta just may be talking to the boss about the boss, listening to the boss talk about the boss, and being a really good audience no matter what the boss is talking about. It's flattering for people to be so interested in you and whatever you have to say, hanging on every word. Plus, the person who is doing those three things is getting a lot of face time and may well be monopolizing the boss's time. And when you have the boss's ear, your story is going to get heard, first and loudest. BAITERs know this all too well.

If all you are ever hearing is what you want to hear,
be afraid. Be very afraid.

#2: They define you as a conspiratorial confidant.

Although BAITERs don't have much in the way of empathy, they are keenly aware of other people's vulnerability and the popularity of the "sport of gossiping." If they discover that their target is willing to gossip, they have found an "in." They exploit this by fostering "conspiratorial relationships"—an "us against them" mentality. You've encountered these people time and again. Everything is a "secret." They can be really obvious, even in terms of body language. They tend to lean in really close, put their hand up by the side of their mouth, presumably to guard the sanctity of the message, and even speak in low tones. Many statements begin with "Did you hear..." or "I've got to tell you something, but you cannot tell a soul." What they're doing is trying to define a relationship on an intimate-disclosure level because they are smart enough to know that they can rely on your "reciprocity." If they engage you in what seems to be an unguarded and private manner with delicate and sensitive information, then you are very likely to accept that definition of the relationship and respond in kind with your own sensitive disclosures. And these BAITERs are correct because we tend to engage people at the level they engage us, so we're likely to respond as *they* intend.

How do they do this? They bait you with *seemingly* intimate life details and experiences in order to suck you in and get you to do the same. For example, someone in your office may tell you about inadvertently seeing your boss having a fight with his wife in the parking lot. "I was surprised," he might say. "I never saw that side of him before. Have you?"

He's baiting you with his conspiratorial sharing. You might respond by engaging him at the same level and telling a story about something your boss did to you. Or you might say—*confidentially,* of course—that you actually witnessed the same scene in the parking lot but didn't want to say anything about it to anybody.

At that point he's got you—you are "dead meat." You have become a partner in crime! By engaging, you have violated a boundary *with a partner,* a partner who will throw you under the bus at the first opportunity. You have put your well-being in his hands, and he is about to crumple it up and throw it away. He's like a cat with a dead mouse waiting to take it back to its owner—the boss of both of you. So the next time he's in a conversation with your boss, he lets slip that *you* were gossiping about the boss fighting with his wife in the parking lot. Or maybe even, to curry both favor and credibility with the boss, he might say something like, "I hate to bring this up, but if there's one thing that I just can't stand, it is disloyalty and vicious backbiting. You need to know that this woman in our department"—*you*—"is spreading poison about your relationship with your wife and your abusive nature. I'm sorry, I'm not one to carry tales, but that just makes me sick to my stomach. Please keep me out of this if you even think it's worthy of your response, because I just don't want to be sucked into this. I love you, and I love my job and this company too much."

So the boss is now furious with *you*, of course. But how are you going to deny that you were gossiping? You actually *were* talking about him behind his back. And now you're toast. If he asks you point blank, "Have you been talking about me and my wife and my abusive nature?" you've got nowhere to run and nowhere to hide. And if you now try to point a finger at your co-worker, you're fighting an uphill and defensive battle because your co-worker got to the boss first.

Do not get sucked in by the hero worship, because it is just a matter of time before those roses they are throwing turn into daggers.

Another word of caution: People who take an extreme position, such as being your new best friend forever, your most passionate ally, your greatest supporter, and your biggest fan and conspiratorial confidant, can be very dangerous. People who occupy one extreme of the emotional continuum are the very ones who tend to flip-flop to the *other* emotional extreme. If someone "sort of" likes you and then changes their mind, that person is likely to "sort of" *not* like you. By contrast, people who put you on a pedestal and hold you in such high esteem, even if it's phony, can have a radical and extreme change of heart. And you and I both know that none of us belongs on that pedestal to begin with, so we are guaranteed to ultimately disappoint and thus wind up with an overzealous enemy. These are often the very people who try to enter into these conspiratorial relationships with you. So do not take the bait. Do not get sucked in by the hero worship, because it is just a matter of time before those roses they are throwing turn into daggers.

#3: They are way too focused on getting your approval—as though their very existence depends on your accepting them.

When I was in clinical practice, one red flag that got my attention was clients who were too concerned about what I thought rather than finding a solution to the problem that brought them into my office. If you have a problem and are sincere about fixing it, you want to focus on it: You're depressed, your wife has had an affair, or your son is on drugs. You're not trying to impress your counselor; you don't care whether he likes you. You want help with your problem. So you should be looking for action steps, not watching the therapist out of the corner of your eye to see who's winning favor and who's getting blamed.

Be very cautious of someone who seems to be "working you" rather than working the problem.

But BAITERs are terribly insecure, so they are always trying to win allies and supporters. They have a need to win you over that goes beyond just forming a relationship as I described earlier. The BAITERs need for you to actually endorse their position, whatever it may be, because they will use you to validate them at some point. Don't be surprised to hear they have told someone, "Carol agrees with me 100 percent! She thinks you are dead wrong, too." They're looking for your approval, constantly checking on your reaction so they can use it to con someone else.

Be very cautious of someone who seems to be "working you" rather than working the problem. You might miss their manipulations because you are so busy working on their problem, trying to help them, while they are busy trying to screw you!

#4: They are always gathering data and "building a file" on you. Everything they do, every interaction, is for a purpose.

The infiltrating flatterer, the co-conspirator, and the approval seeker I've been talking about all have one thing in common. They're always trying to discover as much about you as they can so they can use the information against you or bolster themselves in some way. They're testing you the way horses test an electric fence—looking for flaws, weaknesses, vulnerabilities, and a way inside.

But this means they're never genuinely engaged because they always have a hidden purpose and are always at a distance from your interaction, rather than truly being part of it. Constantly thinking this way takes time and energy away from spontaneous human connection. The BAITER can't engage in the normal back-and-forth of a social exchange, because he's too busy thinking about what information he can obtain for leverage.

He can give the *appearance* of being engaged, but his flattery, attempts at seduction, and approval-seeking should give him away. With proper sensitivity, you will quickly discern when you are being pumped for information. In fact, if you will pay attention to the areas of inquiry, you may even gain insight into what the "setup" is likely to be. At the risk of making you paranoid, my advice is that you have to be very careful of what information you are giving someone and think about how that information, taken out of context or "spun up" by a manipulator, could come back to haunt you. Sometimes the information they gather can be even more valuable than money. For example, the BAITER will pump you to find out your values and what you passionately believe in so that when the time is right, he can mimic those positions, claiming them as his own in order to bond with you and gain your trust. When he gains your trust, he gains access to you and your life.

And remember, you are potentially dealing with a BAITER, someone with a nefarious, self-serving, and potentially destructive agenda. You may be thinking they have no reason to try to hurt you. But these people don't need a "rationale"; they only need to believe that derogating or undermining you will somehow advance their cause. They are looking to taint or eliminate competition, and you don't want to give them the very ammunition that might well bring you down.

#5: They consistently misdirect and maintain a mystery about who they really are; they answer questions that weren't asked; they obfuscate.

People who have nothing to hide, hide nothing. BAITERs have plenty to hide, because I am willing to bet that you are not their first target or potential victim. They will frequently avoid responding directly in any discussion that requires them to take a personal position, be specific about their past, make a substantive self-disclosure, or make a commitment that could come at a cost or narrow their options. If they "sign on" to back you or support some position that narrows their ability to flip-flop and jump on the bandwagon of a yet-to-be-determined winner, they will get as nervous as the pig who knows he's dinner.

People who have nothing to hide, hide nothing.

Did you ever have the experience of trying to steer a conversation back to the subject at hand while the person you're talking to seems determined to take it in an irrelevant direction? This is another tactic of the BAITERs. They obfuscate by focusing on irrelevant details and *answering questions that weren't asked.* This is an easily observable behavior, so be especially on the lookout for it. We have all seen this happen with children who have something to hide.

Mom: "Hey, Billy, what's up? Are you and your little friend having fun playing out in the yard?"

Billy: "Yes, and we aren't playing with matches, OK!"

Mom: "Whoa! Hold on there, Seabiscuit! What's this about matches?"

Busted. BAITERs do it all the time, just like little Billy.

You've been around long enough to know when you are having a genuine and authentic conversation with someone. But until now, you may have just thought other people were scatterbrained or airheads when they just didn't seem to be able to grasp the heart of the matter. What I'm telling you is that sometimes people like this know exactly what the heart of the matter is, and they know exactly how to obfuscate. Pinning them down is like trying to "sack fog" or nail Jell-O to the wall. You can get close, but you just can't quite get it done. Now, you at least have a new theory as to why.

#6: When confronted with problems, they always blame others.

BAITERs always want to make sure you understand whose fault it was, and it's seldom theirs. They do not take accountability or ownership for anything of negative consequence.

But you know better than that. There's seldom a problem that's 100 percent the responsibility of one side and zero percent the other. Relationships are mutually defined. Maybe it's 90/10,

80/20, 50/50, whatever—the question is always, what's *your* role in this? What's *your* ownership of the problem? If the BAITER gets a DUI, the cops were unfair, it was a setup, someone must have drugged their beer, the Breathalyzer was wrong. Somebody besides them is responsible for their getting in trouble. If they get caught having an affair, "She came on to me!" (As if that matters to you!) "I didn't even know what was happening; I was drunk." (As if *that* matters to you!)

They are never wrong, never responsible, never accountable, and never willing to step up and own their part in a negative situation.

This is a major problem because people cannot change what they don't acknowledge. The BAITERs acknowledge nothing, so they change nothing. You cannot expect these people to have some moment of insight and begin to hold themselves to a higher standard. It is simply not going to happen, and if you are in their life, you will become a target of blame. They are never wrong, never responsible, never accountable, and never willing to step up and own their part in a negative situation. Guess what? Somebody must be to blame, and since it is *never* them, that leaves you. Enjoy your time under the bus because that's right where you're headed when you deal with BAITERs.

At the absolute most, they use calculated "modified *mea culpas*" to *seemingly* admit responsibility or take accountability on a safe, miniscule, and irrelevant part of a problem. But that's just deflection, not genuine ownership of a problem. Oftentimes these "modified *mea culpas*" are in fact self-praise in disguise.

The master manipulator will find a way to narcissistically compliment himself or herself, all the while disguising it as taking ownership in a problem.

If the BAITER is caught red-handed physically abusing his wife, he will justify it: "If I allowed her to go off on me like that, I'd be cheating her." In other words, he's actually doing something good by abusing her. He's *helping* her. If he didn't abuse her, he'd be letting her down, failing to take what he sees as his responsibility to draw the line.

Deflection, deflection, deflection. These guys are good. You have to be better.

#7: They lie, either by misstatement or by omission; they understand that lies with a kernel of truth are the most powerful.

Everybody lies. You do it, I do it, and everyone you know does it at some point. So, why is this in the BAITER's "playbook?" Because you and I are amateurs! When I say "lie," I'm not talking about a husband who swears to his wife that "those jeans" do *not* make her look fat when in fact he is thinking "Whoa! It looks like two pigs playing under a blanket! But those are the tenth pair of jeans she has tried on, and we are already 20 minutes late." Failing to share that little tidbit is a lie by omission (and also a life-saving "edit"). When a BAITER lies, however, it is all too often for a very nefarious purpose and designed to mislead someone who, if they knew the truth, would likely behave very differently. The BAITERs' lies are, by design, material misrepresentations that they are counting on you to accept as truth. Therein is the power of their lies.

BAITERs are masters at three types of misdirection: affirmative misstatements ("I saw him kissing her"), lies by omission (failing to tell you what they really saw or didn't see), and "half-truths" ("I saw him kissing a blonde at the airport," but failing to tell you it was his sister, which he well knew because he was introduced to her and had seen her before!), all of which give you a false picture of reality. Because they have no conscience to struggle with and have had a lot of practice, they are good, really good. They are committed liars who will stick with the lie to the point of destruction, if need be. Many times, as I mentioned earlier, when they are in the actual moment of the telling, they may actually believe what they are saying, at least at some level. They immerse themselves in the role-play, like skilled actors. Daniel Day Lewis is known for being a dedicated method actor, and it's been said he's done everything from living off the land for six months when he starred in *The Last of the Mohicans* to being spoon-fed by the crew while playing a character with cerebral palsy. BAITERs love the drama of the role-play and feed on the exhilaration of the lie. If they are playing the role of victim in the lies, they can actually feel sorry for themselves!

Because they have no conscience to struggle with and have had a lot of practice, they are good, really good.

The BAITERs are also good because they pay attention to what you seem to respond to the most, and they will hammer those points. They embed a verifiable "kernel" of truth to gain credibility to the overall story. They will often misdirect by confessing to a lesser offense if it distracts you from their more egregious transgression.

People who have nothing to hide, hide nothing. BAITERs hide everything with a menagerie of lies that would boggle the rational mind.

#8: They are frauds; they cheat, and they steal property, information, and credit for other people's work and claim false competencies to gain trust and reliance.

I was taught in first grade that you don't take what isn't yours, you don't copy off your neighbor in class, and you don't allow someone to think you have achieved something you did not. Contrary to what many seem to think, and the misguided credo BAITERs live by, my parents taught me that the world did not owe me a living. My parents taught me that you work for what you want, rather than expect it to be given to you. BAITERs apparently missed those lessons. Among their tactics is the simple pattern of taking, not earning, what they want. Their behavior is based on the belief that you get a free ride any time you can. If people are dumb enough to leave themselves open to exploitation, if they "allow" themselves to be defrauded, well, then too bad for them; they got what they deserved. And it is hard for non-BAITERs to wrap their heads around how elaborate a fraud they will build. It seems as if, had they worked that hard at something legitimate, they would have been a great success! I once had a guest on the show who went to such great lengths to convince his mistress that he truly was leaving his wife that he actually procured a false set of divorce papers, filled them out in great detail, forged signatures, stamped them, and handed them to her, all to suck her further into his lie. Fraud all the way—and he made no apology for it when he was found out. "You nagged me so much I had to do it." They believe they are entitled to whatever they can get, and the easier, the better. It is the "having" that the fraudster is wholly focused on, not the method of getting. *You* may believe that if you cheat to win, it isn't really a win. To the BAITERs, a win is a win is a win. Earned or stolen is no different to them.

But because they live their lives as a masquerade, they always feel like they're only one step ahead of being found out. This is one of the reasons they have a history of short-term relationships. They have to keep on the move and maintain mystery to avoid being discovered. They never consider that the fraud will eventually "hit the wall" and come crashing down because they lack both foresight and insight. But on a short-term basis, they are great salespeople and can tell a great story and make you believe they are "cutting-edge" competent. They work the sale so hard because they need to disarm you so you don't run off and independently verify their claims, check their references, and otherwise confirm who and what they are. They need to ease your mind so as to kill the need for investigation. Control of the target is essential to any effective fraud, and the BAIT-ERs know it. If they keep you occupied, they can work you from close in.

They have to keep on the move and maintain mystery to avoid being discovered.

#9: They isolate their victims and foster dependency to obligate you and gain leverage and power.

The number-one weapon of abusers in general is isolation. If any BAITERs are "working you," setting you up because you are going to serve a purpose for them or have something they want, they will first attempt to eliminate as many of your other contacts and support systems as possible. They don't want you having any reality checks, encouragement, validation, or differing opinions. They are much too insecure to have others in the mix.

It might be subtle at first, because they just try to be ever-present in your life.

Remember point #1 in this chapter: *They infiltrate your life, seducing with promises and flattery.* Then they will escalate to dominating your time just one-on-one, by always asking you to go to lunch, come over to their house, catch a movie, power-walk in the mornings—anything that gives them a private audience with you. Soon, they will begin to alienate you from others, and others from you. Lies and gossip about others are their favorite tools. If they can get you to believe that others say mean things behind your back, laugh at you, don't like your children, or are sabotaging your career or marriage—whatever your hot buttons are—then they have you in their grips. Healthy relationships have balance and a consistent pattern of give-and-take, with each party receiving no-strings-attached support from one another. BAITERs strive for imbalance, and they achieve that by overdoing for you, going way out of their way for you, so you are in their debt. If any relationship is too one-sided, you should be very wary. I can't tell you how many abused women have told me that in the early stages, their abusers just could not do enough for them. That's because the abuser wants to rope you into his debt and thus his control. Don't be seduced by the BAITER's early service to you and an unwillingness to accept anything in return. You are being set up. As the old saying goes, if it seems too good to be true, it probably is.

Lies and gossip about others are their favorite tools.

They will try to convince you that *"but for them,"* you would be miserable. Without them, you would be lost, alone, incompetent, and downtrodden. I shudder to think how many abusive husbands have, behind closed doors, convinced their abused wives that no one else would ever want her, love her, or even let her stay around. The early helpfulness and giving were never genuine and quickly morphed into control and demand: "I must do this, because you can't! You need me, and I *own* you because you *owe* me!" If they can convince you that you just can't get by without them anymore, they have tremendous leverage that can be used to threaten and intimidate you. "Do what I say or I am gone, and you will be lost and alone."

If you have people who insist or even imply that but for their largesse, you would be lost and alone, people who have actively cut you off from those you once trusted and enjoyed, or people who believed in you and were happy for your success, alarms should be going off in your head right now as you read this sentence.

#10: When in a position of power and authority, they abuse it with self-dealing and egomaniacal conduct.

It has been said that "power corrupts and absolute power corrupts absolutely." This is too often a true sentiment because many people simply don't know how to wield power, and the control goes to their head. With BAITERs, it is an intoxicating circumstance made exponentially worse by their lack of empathy and inability to feel remorse when abusing another. Believing that the world is "theirs for the taking," they will frequently take advantage of a situation and everyone in it in ways that, once discovered, are shocking. To be under the thumb of a power-intoxicated BAITER is a place you never want to find yourself.

Bernie Madoff is a tragic example. He gained people's trust and purse strings. The liberties he took with their money, to the tune of billions of dollars for unprecedented luxuries and lifestyle, destroyed many hardworking people's retirements and even their lives. Once his fraud was discovered, investigators universally asked, "How could he? How could he take the retirement funds of people in their 70s, money from charities that did wonderful work for disadvantaged children, members of his own faith?" The answer should now be, at least in part, clear. He had no ability to feel guilt or sorrow. No ability to comprehend the pain he caused to the elderly or children so that he could buy a third yacht or yet another vacation home. He had way more money than he could ever spend, yet he continued to steal.

The only difference between a Madoff and those in our lives is a matter of scope, a matter of zeros in front of the decimal point. You cannot give them power over you, because they will abuse it and you. If you are working for any BAITERs, you and yours are in harm's way. Get out of denial and start making plans for a change, an escape, right now. It's not a question of "if" but a question of "when" you will be victimized.

#11: They ID your sensitivities and hot buttons to gain leverage.

We all have "hot buttons," and that knowledge in the hands of a BAITER is emotionally dangerous for us. Maybe you have self-doubts or are hypercritical of your appearance, lack of education, or less than stellar past. Whether real or imagined failures and vulnerabilities, the BAITER will pound at you in those areas when he needs you to be less than 100 percent confident. Maybe it's a hot button about child abuse or politics, animal cruelty, or the favoritism your parents showed for one of your siblings. If the BAITER discovers your buttons, I promise you, it goes in their ammo bag, to be pulled out the moment they need to enforce control over you, distract you, or defeat you. A good policy is to share personal information only on a need-to-know basis with new people in your life, until they've earned, and I mean really earned, your trust.

They work to find out what sets you off, and barring that, they will use your general human decency or your concern for them as a lever. It is what I call "emotional extortion." They may threaten that if you leave them or reject them in some way, they will kill themselves, and "their blood will be on your hands!" They will use children as hostages, threatening that if you divorce them or throw them out, they will take the children and live on the streets (a favorite among young mothers mooching off parents or grandparents and resisting helping around the house or refusing to stop drugging or drinking). All of this is designed to induce guilt in you. Feeling guilt is painful, and BAITERs understand that you will do almost anything to escape that pain. These scenarios might sound intense, but remember what I said about much of life boiling down to a war between good and evil. These are just examples of how the battles can play out in your life.

> *We all have "hot buttons," and that knowledge in the hands of a BAITER is emotionally dangerous for us."*

I am hypersensitive about loyalty. It is a standard to which I aspire and to which I hold those in my life. I am highly intolerant of those who are disloyal, either to me and my family or to anyone else for that matter. I see people in Hollywood who work for a major celebrity for years and who, upon having a falling-out or being released from employment for whatever reason, race to write a tell-all book to cash in on the trust and access they once had with the celebrity. I have never, nor will I ever, buy or read one of those books. I have been pitched time and again to have them on the show to "reveal shocking details about the private life of some star." Nope! I'm not interested in having some opportunistic scumbag on my show to betray a former friend or employer. They have no sense of how unbecoming that is to them.

I tell you that story to tell you this one. A definite BAITER infiltrated my family at one point since coming to Hollywood and knew me well enough to know about my loyalty hot button. When he made his "play" to try to get me to feature his product on my show, my professional staff balked. The product wasn't the right fit for the show and would feel out of place. I agreed, and we moved on. This BAITER's reaction was to come at me, armed with tales of disloyalty on the part of specific staff members who had blocked his plans. This person knew of my intolerance of disloyalty and used it to try to move my position and get me to turn a deaf ear to the oppositional thoughts from the people I trusted. He chose his lies carefully and aimed them like a gun.

I have to say he was good, but that little voice in my head was screaming, "Alert! Alert!" It was a voice I might have ignored at one time. Aunt Bee taught me better. He had me in his sights, shot, and missed. His target is still here to this day, but he, on the other hand, looks great in my rearview mirror. Those attempting to leverage you by exploiting your sensitivities and hot buttons will look great in your rearview mirror too.

#12: They have "selective memory" and are revisionist historians; they reframe reality.

Because BAITERs are such consummate liars, they can sometimes completely rewrite history when it serves them, rather than just tell a specific lie. They remember only the details that serve them to recall and simply "forget" the rest. They manufacture or "spin" what they need to in order to support their current position. And as I said, they are committed liars, they are master revisionists, and a lie unchallenged becomes the truth in time. If the BAITER's version is told enough, it can become generally accepted, even by you! (Politicians from both sides of the aisle are experts at this one.)

As the personal revisionist historian rewrites that which he needs to be different, he will simply write you into a role that may have little or nothing to do with what actually happened. If you have found yourself standing there, jaw dropped, thinking you must have gone insane while hearing history rewritten right before you, you aren't insane, but your efforts will be in vain. The BAITER in your life is reframing reality, and you are in the crosshairs. At least now you know how to label it.

I have a friend in Houston who was having some marital discord. His wife thought he was cheating on her, and I'm not sure whether he was or not. But on this day, we were flying in his plane to a business meeting in Washington, D.C. We had to stop by his house on the way to the airport to grab his bags. It was August and unbearably hot and humid, so he said, "Come on in a minute while I get my things, and then we'll be off." We opened the front door, and there stood his wife, Carol, stark naked (don't ask me why—like I said, it was hot, I guess...I don't know!). Now I didn't notice that fact right way, despite her being uncommonly beautiful, because all I could see was the .357 Magnum Diamondback revolver she had cocked and pointed right at us! I knew this woman and knew her to be unstable and deranged. At the risk of sounding judgmental, this woman was also a gold digger of epic proportions, and the way you could tell whether she was lying was if her lips were moving. She was screaming things I can't even write here and shaking with her finger on the trigger. My friend said, "Carol, honey, I know you are upset, but you need to put that gun down, and let's talk like rational adults." I'm thinking, "Beam me up, Scotty!" To fast-forward, she didn't shoot, they did get a divorce, and she made a pretty penny, a very pretty penny.

To your face, they profess their undying loyalty to you. Behind your back, they're poisoning the well.

The point of the story is that when she told her version of the events under oath in a private mediation, it was unrecognizable, to say the least. According to her, her abusive husband had barged in on her naked (kernel of truth) while in the shower, with some jerk buddy of his (me), and backed her into a corner so aggressively she finally picked up a gun to defend herself. Truth is—we never got past the entry hall, and her shower was 30 yards away. She was dry—I, on the other hand, was sweating so much I looked like I'd been in the shower—and she pulled that gun before he ever uttered a syllable. Selective memory and revisionist history by a BAITER with a very specific agenda. You've probably been there, ideally less dramatically, and you probably will be again. Now you know what's going on.

#13: They are two-faced; they spread lies and gossip—pretending to be your friend and ally to give you a false sense of security while being disloyal.

This is a BAITER's tactic that is an especially easy one to see, *if* you embrace one undeniable truth: "If they will do it *with you*, they will do it *to you*!" BAITERs are so narcissistic, they don't realize that you can see right through them when it comes to spreading lies and gossip. If they are standing there trashing someone else to you, it is naïve for you to think they won't then go and trash *you* to someone else. BAITERs believe that undermining those with whom they live and work is just another tool for getting ahead. They believe if they can tear you down in the eyes of others, they will, by comparison, look better. And they will make you think they love you all the while!

They use these character-assassination tactics to recruit allies and attempt to coop or highjack your support system. Their belief is that if they can get those who support you to switch their allegiance to them, then they have strengthened their position and, just as importantly, weakened yours. They will lie about you to create that shift. To your face, they profess their undying loyalty to you. Behind your back, they're poisoning the well.

#14: Because they are paranoid, they "get you" before you "get them."

As my dad said, we can see in others only that which we possess within ourselves. That is why non-BAITERs can't easily see a con man, an abuser, or a crook coming around the corner. It is also why BAITERs assume that if they don't get you, you *will* get them. If you look at it that way, it makes perfect sense for BAITERs to attack, exploit, and victimize everyone they can. For if not, in their mind, they will become the victim. They can't help themselves. Even if everything is running smoothly and everyone is happy, they will cross that line, just because they have that nagging fear that you will take advantage of them. And they *will not* be a sucker for anybody!

Insecure people, even non-BAITERs, are prone to this. Think about it: If Susan believes she won't be accepted into a social circle, a club, a team, or a relationship, she can spare herself the pain of rejection by rejecting them first. She might find fault with the person, people, or group, so she can convince herself that she doesn't want to belong with that group anyway. But someone like Susan will play some seemingly "protective" mind games with herself and then just move on with her life. BAITERs have a different and typically hidden agenda, and they move on to *that* rather than moving on with their life. So, ask yourself, are you failing to see that someone is gearing up to "get you" before you "get them?"

#15: They are masters of passive-aggressive sabotage.

Resistance can be overt and in your face, or it can be subtle and deniable. Passive-aggressive sabotage is on the all-star hit parade list for BAITERs. They *love* this one, because they can do it and not get their hands dirty. Rather than tell you to your face how they feel, they just use "guerrilla warfare" to insidiously undermine all of your efforts.

Jason and Carl are both vying for a leadership position heading up a key project in their division at work. Jason gets the nod to lead the efforts, and Carl, *to Jason's face*, says, "Hey, congratulations, I'm 100 percent behind you! Let's make this work; just tell me how I can help." Carl then passively sets about making sure that there isn't one chance in a million that Jason will succeed. When Carl gets an assignment, he just seems to get confused and makes a mess of it—of course because the instructions were confusing. He miscommunicates with other members of the team, so they mess up. He passively fosters discontent among team members and fans the flames of their concern that they will be blamed. Meanwhile, he tells Jason that, in his opinion, everything is going swimmingly, and he should take a step back and let his team have some autonomy to make them feel a sense of ownership in the project. It's the sign of a good leader: delegate, don't micromanage. Then when the boss shows up looking for Jason, Carl is quick to say, "Who knows? I haven't seen him in forever. And we could sure use some guidance here. We have no idea what the goal is. He has some of us working on one thing and some of us basically undoing what the others did. I mean, I want to help, but I don't feel like I should get in his way. And I really feel like you deserve better. But Jason is such a great guy when he is here."

As I said earlier, my focus here has been more on who they are and what they do than why they do it.

He quietly sabotages Jason and then hides the damage until it's too late to recover, throws him under the bus behind his back with staff and superiors, and then finishes by saying what a great guy he is while at the same time subtly applying to replace him. Of course, when he sees Jason, he reports only that the boss is really upset but that he told the boss what a great guy Jason is and covered as best he could. And not one time is Carl on the record in any accountable way! It is gutless, it is insidious, and it is very effective.

Would a Friend Treat You Like That?

Yet another way to understand if, in fact, you are dealing with a BAITER is to ask yourself how a *true* friend would behave. What a BAITER does is exactly the opposite of that. A true friend wouldn't lie to you, cheat you, or steal from you. A true friend wouldn't take credit for work you did. A true friend wouldn't throw you under the bus when there are problems.

There actually may be some genetic components to the behavior of people who fit the BAITER profile. Unfortunately, the research is inconclusive. As I said earlier, my focus here has been more on who they are and what they do than why they do it.

The roots of behavior are complex. What psychologists have learned is that these genetic factors have very likely been reinforced by a number of environmental factors including parent modeling over the years. *Children learn what they live.* If a child grows up with a parent who takes pride in "beating the system" or consistently cutting corners, taking advantage of friends and acquaintances, or even outright committing crimes, the child uses those behaviors as a reference point. The most powerful role model in any child's life is the same-sex parent, so if sons watched their fathers cheat, abuse, and exploit, they are at high risk for following in their fathers' footsteps. If daughters watched their mothers do the same thing, even entering into conspiracies to "lie to dad about what we bought" or hide the real magnitude of problems, that behavior can become well-learned.

By the time these BAITERs reach adolescence after having been exposed to this poor modeling, they've learned that all the patterns of behavior we've been discussing in this chapter—the strategy and tactics of the secret "playbook"—have actually helped them get what they want.

This is one reason BAITERs are so resistant to therapy. Counseling doesn't always change their behavior; in fact, it sometimes reinforces it by enabling them to learn the symbol system of therapist, to describe the world in the language the therapist understands—in other words, therapy sometimes just teaches these BAITERs how to be better at what they do. It teaches them how to describe what they do so they can manipulate the people who are supposed to be helping them. They are being taught what sells. Their therapists are modeling for them how to mimic empathy, remorse, caring, and feeling.

Don't be fooled: Sometimes people who are the most artic-ulate in the language of therapy are just using it to advance their own interests. It's just one more tool in their arsenal of manipulation. It creates the fictional awareness of insight, but it's just encouraging you to draw a false conclusion about them.

The next time your gut instinct warns you about someone, don't just hear what they are saying; really listen to their words. Are the words authentic, or are they just a "line?" And remem-ber, actions speak louder than words. No amount of excuses and rationalization can cover repeated conflicts with authority, bankruptcies, defaults, or jail records. No amount of psycho-babble can excuse bad behavior.

A true friend wouldn't lie to you, cheat you,
or steal from you.

Just like a teenage girl on her first date, you've got to learn all the pick-up lines ahead of time so you won't fall for them when the first guy springs them on you. And you don't have to feel bad about saying no.

As I said in Chapter 2, it probably wouldn't be very hard to think of a list of the people who have violated you. Now that you have a clear understanding of BAITERs' traits and tactics, it's time to make this list.

RECOGNIZE POTENTIAL THREATS

In the following chart, write down the people in your current life who you fear are out to sabotage you or take what is yours and leave you in the dust. Next, write down which of the "Nefarious 15" they're attempting to use against you. It could be one, or it could be several.

POTENTIAL BAITER	NEFARIOUS 15 TACTIC USED

Now you've just greatly lowered your risk of being blind or blindsided by potential BAITERs in your world. Remember, an egocentric point of view justifies everything. BAITERs with no empathy will take advantage of every opportunity that comes their way. You can't be naïve and self-protective at the same time. You can't take a Scarlett O'Hara mentality: "I don't want to think about that today; I'll think about that tomorrow." You've got a problem today. You need to be vigilant today.

To win in the real world and protect what's yours, you have to be willing to ask distasteful questions of other people and of yourself. I would rather suspect ten innocent people temporarily than fail to uncover one snake that could do permanent damage to me or those I love.

A Note to the BAITERs Among Us

If the first three chapters of this book have read like your autobiography, if in reading it, you feel like I actually know you and am describing you, then I have some things to say especially to you. First and foremost, life is about choices, and if you are a BAITER, if you spend your life jerking people around, it is because you're choosing to do so. You're not a victim, you're not a "genetic prisoner," and you're not captive to your upbringing. If you can choose to do it, and you can, you can most certainly choose not to do it. The biggest problem you face is that you have a distorted perception that what you're doing is in fact working. But, it isn't working. It isn't even almost working.

You see, people who behave the way I have described in Chapters 1, 2, and 3 are generally thought to be suffering from some type of personality disorder. That means they are mentally and emotionally ill, they are not thinking right, they are not feeling right, and they aren't making sound decisions. These people, including you, if the description fits, tend to be resistant to treatment because, as I have said, their misperception is that what they're doing is actually working for them. BAITERs are typically very immature, and immature people tend to seek immediate gratification without consideration for long-term implications. You can sometimes get a short-term payoff if you get away with exploiting someone. So, in the moment, on an immediate basis, it can appear that what you're doing is working. But if you step back and take the "long view," you can see that, throughout your life, you have never built any relationships that are lasting, you never achieve anything that you are genuinely proud of, and you never have a sense of peace because you are always immersed in drama, conflict, and turmoil because people object to you exploiting them.

Another reason making a change is an uphill battle is that you are very likely so narcissistic that you really do think you're smarter than everybody else and you think your current lifestyle of using, abusing, manipulating, and hurting people is in fact a "cool" or smart way to live and to get you what you want. But I'm betting you don't have any real friends—how could you, because all you see are suckers and targets? I'm also betting that if you are honest, you admit to being lonely and oftentimes feel as though you're one step ahead of getting found out and caught. Sorry, but my question is, "Who is the sucker here?" That is not what I would call a successful lifestyle.

So, if I'm describing you and you want more, then decide that you're going to make a change. Decide you're going to earn what you have in this life instead of stealing it. Decide you are going to make a "to-do" list about developing such things as empathy and honesty and compassion. And while you're making that "to-do" list, let me suggest an item that should go right at the top. You need to figure out why you feel so bad about yourself that you think you can't have any success in this life without stealing it, conning somebody out of it, or perpetrating a fraud to trick them into giving it to you. You see, if you had confidence in who you are and what you have to offer, then you would have confidence that good things could be created by you and enjoyed by you, because you are worthy and deserving of them.

Now, I know that even though you have read this note, you may still believe you are the smartest person in the world and you can completely blow it off, but I can assure you, now that you have read it, now that it's in your brain, it may very well haunt you for the rest of your life until you do something about it. I say that because I am telling you now, unequivocally, that your life is empty and you have to look over your shoulder every day to be sure you're not in some way held accountable by somebody you took advantage of. You will get tired of that if you're not already, and you will remember me saying you have a choice to do differently. You have a choice to come off the shady side of the street and start walking in the sunlight. It takes guts, but the payoffs are huge. And, it's not nearly as much work because you don't have so much to remember. The truth doesn't have versions; it just is.

Make a choice right now to stop the manipulation, become transparent, and earn mental health and well-being in your life by doing the things you need to do. If you need professional help, get it. And here's a great piece of advice, if I do say so myself: Begin by telling your therapist the worst of the worst about you. If you're a cheating, stealing, manipulative liar who exploits anybody you can get to, then tell your therapist. Tell them you want nothing short of transparency because you realize that your tendency is to con them too. "Man up!" Do the right thing and give yourself a chance and the rest of us a rest because we are beyond tired of dealing with your crap. I wish you the best of luck if and only if you commit to making the changes. I hope you do. Take the high road; there's a lot less traffic up there.

Part 2

The New "Life Code" and Rules for Winning in the Real World

4

Stop Being a Target

*"You can call me a S.O.B., but you
are going to do it long distance!"*

—Dr. Phil McGraw

Okay, enough about the bad guys. I want to shift gears and talk about you and your positive power, positive choices, and creating the positive outcomes in your life that you want and deserve. You now know who the bad guys are and how they do what they do. That is knowledge the new "Life Code" requires you to have to be effective, and it will help you inoculate yourself against their attacks and intrusions. Knowing everything you possibly can about the people who can become your and your family's enemies is critically important to changing your experience of life going forward. But what is even more critically important than them is *you*. That's really good news, by the way, because the only person you need to control to create the results you want is you, which works out especially well because the only person you *can* control is you.

To be maximally effective, you need to learn how to play smarter and harder and bigger in every aspect of your life. Barring catastrophic illness or fatal accident, anybody can *live*, but living effectively, living fully, and getting the biggest "bang for your buck" in this life is a whole other story. My goal in the rest of this book is to empower you to function as the highest and best version of yourself. To stop being a target, to avoid being low-hanging fruit just waiting to be pulled down, you have to take a long, hard look at yourself and how *you* play this game of life. To do otherwise is tantamount to volunteering to be used and abused. I contend that you can and must do more, regardless of how often you do or do not encounter BAITERs. I don't want you to leave anything "on the table," so to speak. I want you to have the full experience and score the biggest win possible.

To be maximally effective, you need to learn how to play smarter and harder and bigger in every aspect of your life.

It's one thing to be naïve (though you can't use that excuse if you've made it this far in the book). It's another thing to choose to behave in such a way as to offer yourself up as a target, as a victim. Why is that?

Someone who's naïve is just ignorant. I know that sounds harsh, but "ignorant" doesn't mean "stupid." It simply means there are things you don't know. I'm perfectly willing to admit I'm ignorant when it comes to the management of toxic biological agents, for example. If you tell me, "Hey, we have a bactcrial outbreak in Central LA. It's spreading like wildfire—what do you think we should do?" Call the CDC, because I'm not your guy. But if you ask me how to get over a breakup or how to deal with addiction, pull up the couch because I'm your guy. But I'm smart enough to acknowledge my areas of ignorance and consult an expert when I need help concerning things I know nothing about. And the fact that you're reading this book means you're taking steps to learn how to create a better life for yourself and those you love.

And by the way, if you feel like your life is working pretty well, by all means read on. Research across decades has been very consistent in showing that psychology works best for those who need it least. That really makes sense if you think about it. Those whose lives are already working pretty well probably have some degree of momentum, an open mind, a willingness to learn, and the confidence to try new things. Compare that to someone who is so dysfunctional that they hide from the world in an "emotional fetal position." Those folks don't have the same tools to work with or the foundation to build on. In fact, I'm betting if you're reading this book, there are many things in your life that are working that you can use as a springboard to take you to the next level. My guess is that you want to and are ready to become a "mover and shaker" in your life. That means taking some risk and trying some new, different things. It's all about being your own "change agent."

I'm betting if you're reading this book, there are many things in your life that are working that you can use as a springboard to take you to the next level.

Being a victim, however, is different from being a change agent. It can be a "comfort zone," a way of never having to put yourself on the line. It can be an excuse. Think about it; if you're a victim, if you have a sad story to tell and you are always ready to tell it, then people feel sorry for you and make excuses for why you aren't doing better in life. That excuse can come in pretty handy if you're someone who's been flat-out unwilling to put it on the line and create what you want in your life, while complaining about what you don't have in your life. There's an old saying that goes, "There are no victims, only volunteers." BAIT-ERs are always on the lookout for volunteers, for people who are out of touch with the world—and with themselves. People who feel sorry for themselves, blame others, and simply don't expect to have other than the most mediocre of lives. These people are "easy pickings" and virtually offer themselves up to be exploited.

Define What's Working and What Isn't

The first step in *not* being a volunteer, *not* being a victim, is to really examine yourself and your behaviors so you can make a "to-do" list about what to keep and build on, what to eliminate, and what to acquire in terms of life skills and strategies.

WHAT I NEED TO START, STOP, AND CONTINUE IN MY LIFE

In this chart, list the following: the behaviors or habits you need to *stop* doing because they are disrupting your life, the things you need to *start* doing because their absence is leaving a big void in your life, and the things you need to *continue* doing because they are creating value in your life.

STOP DOING	
	_____
	_____
	_____
	_____
START DOING	_____
	_____
	_____
	_____
CONTINUE DOING	_____
	_____
	_____
	_____

This task isn't just about avoiding being exploited. It is also, maybe even more so, about what you're actively doing for *you*. Trust me, you can go through your life having never been victimized by anyone and still not even come close to getting what you want for you and yours. That happens because you don't have the skills needed to aspire for more, the willingness to even admit that you want more, or the guts to actually go for it. If you want *more* in your marriage, *more* in your social life, *more* in your spiritual life, *more* in your career, or just *more* in your life across the board, common sense tells you that you have to go after it with *more* passion and commitment. I am one of those who believes the fruit we must reach for is much sweeter than that which falls at our feet. Reaching, stretching, and trying new things is good for us. It keeps us moving and growing. And similarly, if you want less of some things such as stress, conflict, or loneliness, you need the same passionate commitment.

Remember, what you are trying the hardest to hide is exactly what you broadcast about yourself the most.

Life tends to pick up momentum whether it's in a positive direction or in the rut of complacency and negativism. And momentum resists change; it wants to keep flowing like a river within its banks. Getting a river to make a right turn is not an easy proposition, and neither is creating major change in the direction of your life. But, it *is* doable.

To do any or all of that, you need to consciously acknowledge that you want more because you cannot change what you do not acknowledge. The first step is getting to know yourself on an intimate level; I mean really, honestly come to know your strengths, weaknesses, and proclivities. Empowerment starts with you. Remember, what you are trying the hardest to hide is exactly what you broadcast about yourself the most. If, for example, you secretly feel superficial, ashamed, insecure, or pride-driven, those self-beliefs will "bleed" through, and sometimes the harder you try to hide them, the more obvious they become. There is wisdom in the words of Shakespeare, "The lady doth protest too much, methinks." But imagine the possibilities if you would just try as hard to *change* as you do to *hide*.

The question is: Do you know your own guilt, shame, fears, doubts, rage triggers, false personas, and insecurities? It is one thing to try to hide things from others, but if you hide the conscious truth from yourself, if you're in denial, you're just sabotaging yourself, because those traits and characteristics you most want to hide and deny will pop up or as I said, bleed through, at the most inopportune times. When the pressure is on, when you need to be at your best, is precisely when denied realities come to bear.

I want you to list the ten things that you would most dread for someone to find out about you. This is for your eyes only, so you can be totally candid. These are the ten things that you'd be most ashamed of and hate the most if someone were to find them out. And if someone were to find them out, they might gain incredible leverage over you. You might think of things that make up a shameful past or a painful present. Maybe you're a volunteer for a pro-life organization, but you're ashamed of the fact that you had an abortion many years ago. Or perhaps you're currently hiding debilitating anxieties from your friends and colleagues. Hiding a bankruptcy, a family member who is in prison, or a nervous breakdown are all examples of things that, if found out, BAITERs could use to their advantage and your demise. But if you know these things about yourself, then you can't be shocked and surprised if they're brought to light, because you've already come to grips with them.

CONFRONT WHAT YOU'RE HIDING

Write down the ten things about yourself that you're hiding from others. Be totally honest!

1. _____

2. _____

3. _____

4. _____

5. _____

6. _____

7. _____

8. _____

9. _____

10. _____

The upside is this: If you have the guts and willingness to get totally real with yourself about yourself, you will have a huge advantage over everybody still stuck playing head games with themselves. More importantly, you can't be ambushed. You've dealt with the issue already. Your ultimate goal is to accept yourself, flaws, fallacies, and all, and then forgive your failures and start fresh. That's what this list gives you the power to do. Don't you feel better having acknowledged these things, having gotten them out and said them, even if only to yourself? Think about it: Even if you have a serious illness like cancer, aren't you better off once you know—I mean really know—the diagnosis, prognosis, and challenges of treatment? Don't you feel better once you've accepted the truth and all it entails?

The same is true about who you are and are not. If you have a hole in your boat and you're pretending like you don't, you're still going to sink. So now you've gotten real with yourself about yourself. No social mask, no spin, no defensiveness—just straight-up truth. The truth is a powerful thing; it really will set you free from emotionally distorted fantasies that paralyze you and make you so easy to exploit

Now that you've been honest about who you are, you've discovered what you're capable of, and you more clearly see where you're vulnerable. You might not be able to change all of those realities, but if you acknowledge them, you won't panic when they come into play. I believe that half the solution to any problem lies in defining it first and then getting all of your resources on the table so you know what you're working with. Now that your resources are on the table, you can understand whether or not you're dialed into the real world.

Play the "What If?" Game

Maybe you were nodding your head as you read the previous chapters and recognized someone you know, some BAITER who's been in your life or in the life of someone you love. But have you been nodding your head as you've been reading *this* chapter? Are you brave enough to look in the mirror and truly see yourself as someone who is vulnerable to self-sabotage? That is the heart of the challenge here because, as I said, it is not only the BAITERs who can get in your way; you can get in your own way.

The hardest part of really getting to know yourself is facing your fears, the ones that keep you awake at night, tossing and turning and staring at the ceiling as the anxiety grips you and brings you to a cold sweat. Anxiety is one of the biggest obstacles to success in anyone's life. If you so much as admit to yourself that you want more than you currently have, you can experience a tremendous amount of anxiety. Why? Because once you've admitted that what you have now is not what you want, how can you ever be satisfied staying where you are? Just admitting it to yourself puts pressure on you to try for something more. And in almost every situation, for you to have more, for you to have a greater degree of success, the world and, more specifically, the people in it have to accept and value what you have to offer. And when you put yourself out there, you're risking something. If you're like most people, your number-one fear is rejection, and your number-one need is acceptance.

If you're like most people, your number-one fear is rejection, and your number-one need is acceptance.

Think about asking the one you love to take your relationship to the next level. Marriage? Exclusivity? Living together? This is anxiety-producing because your special someone might look at you and say, "Gee, I'm so sorry, but I'm afraid I'm going to have to say no." Ouch! After admitting you wanted more, after putting yourself out there and asking to be accepted and validated, you are told that you are just not enough, and the sting of rejection and failure can last a long, long time.

Because you know that is a possible outcome, you can be paralyzed by anxiety and fear of rejection. You can be stuck in a very uncomfortable "comfort zone." And what do we all do when we are faced with potential rejection or failure? We begin to play the "what if?" game.

You've done it a million times—you know you have.

"What if he doesn't like me?"

"What if I sing in front of everyone and they hate it?"

"What if I try to have a child and find out I can't?"

"What if I tell my significant other I'm not willing to be treated this way anymore, and he just tells me, 'Tough—if you don't like it, get out'?"

"What if I work really hard to write a book about the new 'Life Code' and everyone hates it and nobody even bothers to read it?"

I could go on and on, because there are an infinite number of examples. I'm not so grandiose as to think that I can get you to stop playing the "what if?" game. But it is this mind-set that probably constitutes the single biggest obstacle to your making a significant change. It's probably part of our "emotional DNA." What I can do instead is teach you *how* to play the "what if?" game so you don't wind up paralyzed in your life.

Think of it as a schematic. If A happens, it leads to B. If B happens, it leads to C. If C happens, then D, and so on. But here's the trick: If you're going to play the "what if?" game, then you have to play it all the way to the end. Answer every question until you reach the absolute bottom line. Let's say it takes you from A all the way to E. So what you really have to decide from the outset is whether you can deal with E. I'll apply this schematic to an example. A few years back, I had a delightful woman on my show who was a classically trained pianist. She had experienced a debilitating panic attack during a performance and, as a result, had been unable to sit down and play the piano for years. Here is a paraphrase of our dialogue as I recall it:

HER: What if I sit down and play a piano, especially in front of an audience, and have another panic attack? (*That's A.*)

ME: Okay, let's assume that happens, then what?

Her: I might get nauseated, throw up all over the keys, and then pass out and in front of everyone. (*Now we've got B.*)

ME: Okay, then what would happen?

HER: I would slide off my bench and be passed out on the ground. (*This is C.*)

ME: Okay, then what would happen?

HER: Well (now she's having trouble because she's never played it out this far), I guess, I don't know, I guess, I would lay there, unconscious, until I woke up? Then I would run off the stage, I don't know! (*There's our D.*)

ME: Okay, so you eventually wake up and run off, and then what would happen?

HER: Well, I would be backstage, embarrassed, having confirmed that I had a panic attack problem associated with playing the damn piano. (*And, we've arrived at F.*)

ME: Okay, so the worst that could happen is that you would pass out in front of a bunch of people you don't know and will never see again and wind up backstage knowing what you already know—which is you have a problem with panic attacks and pianos. Have I got that about right? (Now that she's played it out to finality, she can deal with that, rather than all the steps in between.)

HER: Yes, but when you put it that way, it doesn't seem so bad.

ME: Bingo! Exactly my point. The worst that can happen is that you're right back where you are right now (E). You're no worse off, other than a little vomit on your dress. But the upside is that you can observe yourself mastering your fear and reconnecting with the greatest passion in your life, which is playing piano. It seems to me that's a pretty good risk-to-reward ratio, especially since we have already done some very sophisticated treatment of your tendency to panic. If you do it my way, you have at least *a chance* of winning, but in your strategy, you have no chance of winning. So the choice is chance of winning versus no chance of winning. So what do you want to do? Come on, Lassie could figure this one out!

My point to her was pretty simple. Monsters live in the dark. When you turn on the bright lights, what you fear is not nearly as horrible as you made it out to be in the dark, anxiety-riddled fantasy of your mind. If the worst that can happen is that you're right back where you were before you started, you really haven't lost any ground. And maybe you can do an autopsy on why things didn't work, which will prepare you to make a better run at your goal the next time. And of course, you at least have a chance of overcoming the problem and being free of it. There's not much downside, but a huge upside. That is a risk-to-reward ratio that works every time. So if you play the "what if?" game, play it all the way to the end. And when you do, I'm going to bet that once you identify the *real* threat, the real downside, you will decide, "Hey, I can handle that; I'm sure not getting any better sitting on the sidelines." I will confess that although I am in the public eye daily, I am not one of those people who has a need to be loved by strangers. So, if you can adopt the same attitude, the prospect of embarrassing yourself in public won't loom quite so large. Works for me, *every day!*

(By the way, for the first time in years, she played and played just fine. There was a little hiccup in the second verse, but nobody knew it but her. She was absolutely inspiring!)

When you turn on the bright lights, what you fear is not nearly as horrible as you made it out to be in the dark, anxiety-riddled fantasy of your mind.

Have Realistic Expectations

Okay, you've committed to acknowledging what your personal obstacles are and identifying your strengths so you build on them, and you have now figured out how to play the "what if?" game to its conclusion. You've learned that facing your fears will probably leave you no worse off than you are already—and maybe even a lot better off. So where do you go from here?

Winners deal with the truth, with reality, and they do not "blow smoke" at themselves. If you truly get real with yourself at every level, then you should have very realistic expectations about what is going to happen as you undertake a challenge. This is critical, because it is not what happens in life that upsets people; it is the violation of their expectations for what is going to happen that upsets them. This is a critical awareness, because while you may not be able to control everything that happens, you can certainly control what expectations you allow yourself to have. If you are completely honest with yourself, then your expectations will not be violated.

We see this all the time in marriages. Merging two lives is a big, big challenge. You have to learn to share lives, routines, money, possessions, and space. No marriage is trouble-free. There are going to be ups and downs, sacrifices to be made, and frustrations that can be very unsettling. If you go into that marriage expecting love notes and flowers every single day when, in fact, your new hubby is a bit of a caveman who communicates with grunts and gestures, you are going to be disappointed. Similarly, if he expects you to meet him at the back door at the end of every day naked with a martini, I'm *guessing* he is going to be sadly disappointed...maybe not, but I'm guessing! If, on the other hand, you both understand that there will be challenges and that that is just the natural, normal progression of combining two lives, then you will each be thinking that things are going pretty much the way they should be. A couple with the first expectancy set might be looking for a good divorce attorney, while a couple with the second, more realistic expectancy might be looking forward to a long and healthy marriage.

If you're not prepared ahead of time, if you don't do your homework, then you're bound to be disappointed when reality hits home in any situation. It's the difference between expecting A and getting B versus expecting B and actually getting B. This doesn't mean you have to "settle." All it means is you're setting yourself up for a fall if your expectations aren't in line with reality. You have to know not just whom you're dealing with but who *you* are and what your expectations are.

Do Your Homework and Make a List

Now it's time to take everything you've been reading in this book so far and apply it to anyone and everyone in your life. Do your homework, and *don't lie to yourself* about who they are—or who you are. Good or bad, acknowledge it all for what it is. I know I am repeating myself, but this bears repeating: Winners are amazingly honest with themselves about self, others, and situations. If things are in the ditch, they admit it and admit it immediately, even if they wish it weren't true. Remember what I said earlier in the book: Giving people the benefit of the doubt is not a virtue, no matter how badly you *want* them to be okay. That doesn't mean you should prejudge them negatively. All it means is that you're in a neutral position, suspending judgment until you have enough information.

Winners are amazingly honest with themselves about self, others, and situations.

History is at least as important as current observations. In fact, in my view, the best predictor of current behavior is relevant past behavior. If you want to know whether some guy you are falling in love with is going to cheat on you, the best piece of information you can get is whether he cheated in his last relationship, or the one before that, or the one before that.

Of course, emotion can make you lie to yourself. You can convince yourself that you are different from all those other girl-friends. You are the one he really loves. After all those relation-ships, he has grown so much! People change, right?

People just aren't that hard to figure out—but if, and only if, you take the blinders off and become a student of human nature.

Not so much, really. The statistics are really against you here. For Pete's sakes, that could have been you he was cheating on in the past! What makes you think you're so different from all the other women he's been involved with? If he cheated on them, he'll cheat on you!

And think about that the next time you and your co-workers are chatting at happy hour. If your "friend" at work gossips to you about other people, don't be so foolish as to think she isn't *talking about you* to others, including the same people she is gossiping about to you!

People just aren't that hard to figure out—but if, and only if, you take the blinders off and become a student of human nature. This means paying attention to the habits and patterns of those around you. Don't be distracted by the social mask, the image they are selling. Figure out who they really are by looking behind the veneer, under the mask, and gathering data, from the small-est bit of information to the most meaningful. When everything is added up, it is highly instructive.

For example, I frequently have celebrities on the show, and I'm always curious who they really are and what they're really like. Of course, they are all nice to *me*, because I'm the one who's getting ready to interview them, and they tend to see me as relevant, at least in the moment. So how they interact with *me* is not very instructive.

But before I sit down in that interview, I take time to talk to my staff. I want to know how the "it" girl or guy I'm about to interview treated the driver who picked them up at the hotel. I want to know how they dealt with the makeup artist and wardrobe person who were helping them get ready for the show. I want to know how they treated the interns and the guy sweeping up backstage.

Those pieces of information, which don't comprise more than two or three minutes of data gathering, can tell me volumes about who a person really is. If they're sweet, warm, and cordial to me but condescending, rude, abusive, dismissive, or downright evil to people they regard as beneath them, that tells me two things: First, they can be charming; after all, they're turning it on for me. Second, they can mistreat people who don't matter to them. This is important information that I can gather by just paying attention and asking the right questions of the right people.

Once you've done your homework, then you can adjust your expectations accordingly. And if your expectations of people are consistent with who they really are and if your expectations of how they behave are consistent with what you actually get from them, then you won't be upset, you won't panic, and you won't make a mistake in dealing with whatever they throw your way. If you do your homework, instead of saying, "How could they?" you will be saying, "Yeah, right, boy did I see that coming! They are as predictable as death and taxes!" This is true whether you're dealing with a really big jerk or a wonderful friend who you can count on. The key is to be accurate and realistic, good or bad. Also, while you are at it, grade your own paper as to how you treat the people you don't have to be nice to. Are you a condescending, self-important diva, or are you warm and considerate to everyone, including the people who can't help you? It's an interesting little self-audit, don't you think? This commitment to reality is not just about other people—you also need to be totally honest about yourself. Another audit I think you should do is a "treasure hunt" of sorts. I want you to identify all of the good things about yourself. This is not just an egomaniacal, "hooray for me" exercise in self-aggrandizement. Trust me; it is wrongheaded to believe that focusing on your strengths, skills, and abilities is egotistical or narcissistic. You have to know what you are capable of, what your "go-to" qualities are, so you can nurture those qualities and trust yourself in critical moments. It is good to work on your strengths. My best (least bad!) shot in tennis is my backhand, but even though I have it down pretty well, I work on it regularly to keep it sharp. You should do that with strengths in all areas of your life.

I believe we all have God-given gifts, as well as learned and developed skills. I believe we all make choices about how we treat other people and how we feel about others. So, what I want you to do, all humility aside, is make a list of all your good traits, characteristics, skills, abilities, and God-given gifts.

For example, if you are a really good friend, put that on the list. If you genuinely care about other people and have compassion for their challenges in life, that goes on the list. If you are a superstar when it comes to math (definitely not on my list), put that down. Are you patient? Caring? Dedicated? Tough? All of those, and any other descriptors of what you're proud of, go on your list.

Note: Pay special attention to whether this list is harder to fill out than the list of your shortcomings and problem areas. I'm betting you can more quickly pinpoint your negative attributes—they tend to get more airtime. You spend more time thinking about what's wrong with you than what's right with you.

THE TREASURE OF YOU

Use the following chart to write down the ten things you love the most about yourself. These can be your natural talents, acquired skills, or innate abilities.

1. _____

_____

2. _____

_____

3. _____

_____

4. _____

_____

5. _____

_____

6. _____

_____

7. _____

_____

8. _____

_____

9. _____

_____

10. _____

_____

Now you're going to make another list. What are the hardest things to acknowledge about yourself? This list differs from your list of shortcomings in that these are attributes that tend to be more out in the open and obvious to others, rather than information about you that you are constantly trying to keep secret. Maybe you're shy or maybe you procrastinate or maybe you don't have enough confidence. If so, put that on the list. Do you get impatient or short-tempered? Are you distant and emotionally unavailable? Would your friends say you sometimes let them down? Would your boss or your co-workers or your children or your spouse? If so, be honest enough with yourself to put that on your list, too. It is extremely important that you actually write these qualities down so you can refer to these lists later.

These lists are important because the more you know yourself, the more informed and confident you are about who you are, and the more purposeful you can be about overcoming your less-than-favorite qualities. Also, when you already know and have consciously acknowledged what you aren't proud of, you're less vulnerable to the judgment and attacks of other people. If you already know who you are, you won't be shocked that someone is "on to you." Instead of panicking at being "found out," you will be thinking, "Hey, tell me something I *don't* know." If, on the other hand, you are unclear about who you are, what you know, what you're capable of, and what you have to offer, somebody will come along and state their opinion of you as though it were fact, and it's going to get under your skin. If they are right about a sensitive issue, you just got ambushed. If they are wrong and you know it, it won't get to you; it will roll off you like water off a duck's back.

ACKNOWLEDGE NEGATIVE ATTRIBUTES

Use the following chart to write down ten things you don't like about yourself and are difficult to acknowledge.

1. _____

  _____

2. _____

  _____

3. _____

  _____

4. _____

  _____

5. _____

  _____

6. _____

  _____

7. _____

  _____

8. _____

  _____

9. _____

  _____

10. _____

  _____

What Do You Want?

It's not enough just to know yourself. You have to ask yourself, are you working for what you want or for what you don't want? How do you approach your life in general? Are you passive or aggressive? Everyone has a style. Some people you know come in your life like a cool breeze; others blow in like an 80-piece marching band. These are all examples of what I call an "attitude of approach" to life, and even if you don't think you have one, you do. You may think you're just minding your own business, just existing passively in a reactive mode, but that *is* an attitude of approach, too.

What is it you're trying to get? If you don't have something you're working toward, you're making a serious mistake. You have to be goal-oriented. You can be leading the parade, but if you stop marching, your lazy butt is back in the tuba section before you know it. Even if it's your goal to stop marching, to drop out of the parade, that's a goal. So, you need a to-do list, a list of priorities to work on, even if your goal is to work less. Don't just breathe air; figure out what you want. You may want to get off the ever-moving escalator to avoid getting caught in ascendancy, but without a goal, you're like a missile without a guidance system.

You need to be asking what your precise, specific definition of success is. Do you even know? You could have had it all along and not known it, or somewhere along the line you may have passed it by. How would you know if you've been a good parent, a good spouse, a good worker? We used to get grades in school, but no one ever gets a letter grade for parenting. And no one is in a position to really know, except you—if you're being truly honest with yourself.

I've always thought that New Year's resolutions were a little artificial—after all, what's so special about the first day of the year? Why can't we make, and stick to, a resolution made on any given day throughout the year? Still, I think it's a useful exercise to review your past and look ahead to the future, and if that's going to take place on New Year's Day, better than never.

So pretend it's January 1 and ask yourself: Did you achieve what you wanted to last year? If not, why not? Were there unexpected obstacles? Did you lack the discipline or initiative? Some things were out of your control, like the economy or maybe the failure of the business you worked for. Maybe you were laid off, and it had nothing to do with you or how hard a worker you were. But you had some ownership of a lot of other things.

If you don't have something you're working toward, you're making a serious mistake. You have to be goal-oriented.

Have you been having problems in your marriage? Maybe your marriage fell apart. In my book *Relationship Rescue*, I talked about performing an "autopsy" of a failed relationship. How did it die, and why? What was your ownership of the problems that arose? Were there things you should have done that you didn't or things you shouldn't have done that you did? Be honest, and put them all on your list of things to do, or not to do, going forward.

But the to-do list has to be real. Your list has to consist of specific actions toward a realistic outcome, and progress toward achieving the items has to be measurable. That's what makes a goal different from a dream—a goal has a timeline and an action plan. As I said in my book *Life Strategies*, for a dream to become a goal, it has to be specifically defined in terms of operations, meaning what will be done. And you can't have unrealistic expectations, like starting in June and hoping to drop 60 pounds and 10 dress sizes in time for swimsuit season in July. Life changes like that don't just happen; they happen one step at a time. Decide what it is you want. Identify and define your goal with great specificity. Know the answers to the following: What are the specific behaviors or operations that make up the goal? What will you be doing or not doing when you are "living the goal?" How will you recognize the goal when you reach it? How will you feel when you have it?

When I was doing management consulting, the most popular training my company offered was goals acquisition. We went into a work group, and we taught them how to set measurable goals, create action plans for getting there, and hold themselves to a timeline with accountability. All of a sudden, they were meeting goals that the other groups weren't. And all of a sudden, upper management was saying, "Hey, whatever you did over there, I want you to do throughout the rest of the company." Executives went through the same training as their staff; in fact, after they went through it, they "sold" it to their staff because they knew it worked. They knew that having specific goals with a timeline and an action plan is the only way to achieve measurable success in a corporation.

That's what makes a goal different from a dream—
a goal has a timeline and an action plan.

Understanding how businesses work, and how corporate managers are responsible for achieving goals, helped me to see how the same principles should be applied to *self*-management. Say you're in a crumbling relationship, you're over your head in debt, your health is poor, and you're depressed. If somebody else were managing your life, how would you grade his performance? You'd probably fire him! But think about it—*you're* in charge of your life; *you're* your own life manager. You can't fire yourself, but you can do a better job…but only by going through the same kind of goals-acquisition training that executives undertake.

It's like climbing a hill. You can't dream your way to the top; you need to have traction. You have to take one step at a time and dig in with each step. You can measure your progress from the bottom: You're a quarter of the way up at a certain point, then halfway, and so on. And if you get stuck, you have to improve your traction or you have to change your course or you have to put in more effort or maybe you have to stop and take a breath. Whatever it is, you have to figure out where you are, where you want to be, and how to get there—all within a given period of time. That's all that traction is, a better rate of movement from one place to the next. After all, you can't spend your whole life on that hill!

And remember, as your own life manager, you're ultimately accountable to yourself. As I wrote in *Life Strategies*, without accountability, people are apt to con themselves, failing to recognize poor performance in time to adjust and keep from falling short. So consider who in your circle of family or friends might serve as your "teammate," the person to whom you commit to make periodic reports on your progress. We all respond better if we know that somebody is checking up on us and that there are consequences for our failure to perform.

Ask Yourself: What's in It for Me?

That's the kind of question we're typically taught not to ask or at least not to admit to asking. Somehow it seems selfish, egocentric, coldblooded. But actually we ask it every day, all the time. As your own life manager, you have to hold yourself accountable for your own life, your own time. When you turn on my show, I guarantee you'll look at the first five minutes, or maybe just the description on the screen, and ask yourself, "Okay, am I going to watch this or not? What's in it for me? Is this going to entertain me; is it going to improve me? Is it in some way going to enhance my walk through this life?"

Be honest: Everybody, including you, approaches pretty much everything that way. You don't order what you *don't* want at the restaurant—you order what you want, right? You're looking for something that's going to make you happy, going to make you feel good, and going to give you satisfaction. There's nothing wrong with that; it's an inherent characteristic in all of us to approach every situation wondering how it satisfies our self-interest.

Of course, some people will take that to the point of exploiting a situation that others wouldn't. As I said before, that's where their behavior crosses the line from assertiveness to aggressiveness, from protecting themselves to hurting others. But as I also said earlier in the book, you are always "playing politics" because politics are always being played all around you. Even choosing *not* to play is a choice, and that becomes your role in the game.

It's like going to a big crossroads out in the middle of the country. You can go straight ahead or you can go back; you can turn left or you can turn right. Of course, you can always say, "You know what, I just don't want to choose." Well, that's the fifth choice—you can stand there in the middle of the intersection and let life run you right over.

That's a choice. But when you say, "I choose not to play the game," what you're really doing is choosing to play the game poorly. You're choosing to play the game passively. You cannot *not* play.

I recognize that words like "game" and "politics," not to mention "self-interest," are emotionally laden. I get that. But you know what? Most people who react negatively to the idea of life as a "game," as "political," or as nothing but "self-interest" are letting themselves be intimidated by it. When I say, "play the game," it raises a red flag; "politics," a red flag; "self-interest," a red flag. But the truth is, that's life as we know it.

When I was a litigation consultant, one of the lawyers we were working with would try to get something in front of the jury, but the judge would rule it inadmissible. So, he would come back and say, "Well, we didn't get it in, but that jury knows we had something really big." I would say, "Wrong! Juries make their decision based on what they see and hear, not what they don't see and hear, and they did *not* see or hear that piece of evidence you say is so important. At the end of the trial, when they go into the jury room, that will have no impact. So, you better try again and figure a way to get that evidence in, or it's lost." So, they would fight and fight and eventually get it in, and it would turn out that, when the verdict was delivered, it did have a big impact.

Most people who react negatively to the idea of life as a "game," as "political," or as nothing but "self-interest" are letting themselves be intimidated by it.

In the same way, you have to learn how to play the game and advance your self-interest. Don't kid yourself that what you have and what you are don't have an impact. If you want to go through life as a "silent soldier," you will always be a "silent soldier." Do you want to be liked, or do you want to be respected? You can be both, but you have to be willing to stand up for what you want. You have to decide that it is not beneath you to advance yourself. Fighting to position yourself in the best way possible in life doesn't cheapen you or what you do.

I'm betting if you're reading this book,
there are many things in your life that are working
that you can use as a springboard to take you to the
next level.

I've had people ask me, "Dr. Phil, are you a self-promoter?" (I'm pretty sure they meant it as an insult! Ha! Sorry, I wasn't offended.) And my response is, "Good grief, I hope so." Because if I don't believe in myself, how can I expect other people to believe in me? I'm putting up my hand up and saying, "Pick me." When the clock is ticking down, I want the ball. I want to take that last shot. I want to be the go-to guy, and if I'm not willing to stick my hand up and say, "Hey, pick me, and I'll tell you why," then there's something seriously wrong with my personal truth.

You know, I always look at people, and if they're down on themselves, how can I avoid sharing their own opinion? They know themselves better than anybody else, so who am I to second-guess them? If you don't think you have what it takes, if you doubt yourself—well, you know yourself better than I do, so who am I to argue with you? I mean, you apparently know you can't cut it, so why would I think otherwise?

I have given you information that I want you to use to comprise your "attitude of approach" to life. Part of your new "Life Code" is approaching life in a purposeful, proactive way, instead of being reactive. You have to commit to know yourself in terms of your strengths and weaknesses and refuse to be paralyzed by fear and anxiety because the world may not accept or validate you. Trust me, you will be rejected from time to time, but believe in your resiliency, because you do have it. The right attitude and good confidence are necessary but not sufficient. You also need a specific plan and specific skills, and when you have those, you will have an incredible edge in your life.

Think about it: While you are reading this book, doing the work, and getting real with yourself, others might be at home watching a sit-com rerun on television. While you are studying and incorporating the "Life Code" playbook I am about to give you, others might be playing some video game. That's okay for them; this work is *better than okay* for you. Right now I want you to get selfish on your own behalf. I want to empower you in a way that is unique to you—no one else, just you. Bottom line: I don't want you to just be in your life; I want you to *star* in your life. The next chapter is designed to give you the new "Life Code" playbook for doing exactly that. And what makes it unique is that you will apply the truths differently than anyone else.

Your New "Life Code" Playbook

"It is not the critic who counts: not the man who points out how the strong man stumbles or where the doer of deeds could have done better. The credit belongs to the man who is actually in the arena, whose face is marred by dust and sweat and blood, who strives valiantly, who errs and comes up short again and again, because there is no effort without error or shortcoming, but who knows the great enthusiasms, the great devotions, who spends himself for a worthy cause; who, at the best, knows, in the end, the triumph of high achievement, and who, at the worst, if he fails, at least he fails while daring greatly, so that his place shall never be with those cold and timid souls who knew neither victory nor defeat."

—THEODORE ROOSEVELT

During my days as a litigation consultant, I practically lived in trial. We were either in intense preparation or actually in the courtroom duking it out. I always looked at those trials as microcosms or mirrors of the way things happen in life. There were two sides fighting to assert their positions and convince someone with the power to decide that they were right and, thus, deserving of the prize. Each side had a well-defined plan; their key players took purposeful action toward an equally well-defined outcome. And, after what was usually a relatively short period of time, the judge or jury declared someone a winner and someone a loser. I *loved* that part of the process. Psychology can some-times seem "fuzzy" as to both science and outcome. But in that microcosm, there was nothing fuzzy: Either your plan worked and you won or it didn't and you lost, and I loved it.

I believe that all of our lives are made up of a *series* of "trials" or tests and challenges that, when laid end-to-end, comprise the timeline of our existence. Some of these "trials" are declared bat-tles, and some are more subtle—a battle is going on, but no one says it out loud. But whatever the test, you must be a powerfully effective advocate for yourself and those you love, and some-times, beyond advocacy, you must be a formidable combatant.

I believe that all of our lives are made up of a series *of "trials" or tests and challenges that, when laid end-to-end, comprise the timeline of our existence.*

One thing I learned with great certainty during those years spent in trial was that in almost every case, the outcome was determined *and knowable* before either party ever walked through the courthouse door. These disputes were never decided in some Perry Mason fashion. There were no surprises. In a close case, the winning side was typically the side that out-prepared their opponent, had the better plan, and executed it in a more committed and focused manner. What I have observed since is that the same rules apply to our lives in general. If you do your homework, if you prepare, if you have a plan and behave with purpose, you can achieve your goals, and you can win out over those who seek to exploit you and yours.

By now, if you have been doing the self-examination and assignments contained in earlier chapters, you know yourself a lot better than you did before we started. You know what you want to achieve, and you can spot and understand unscrupulous people who may get in your way and try to sabotage you from time to time. But understanding yourself and others is not enough. The universe rewards action, and you must create your own playbook as an integral part of the new "Life Code" we have been talking about.

If I said I wanted you to pinpoint and describe the rules and tactics in your current "playbook for life," would you have one, even in your head, to refer to, or do you live more in reactive mode when things call for it? Would you know what to write if you wanted to pass your philosophy on to your children? And if you did come up with your current "code" by which you live, how is it working for you? I have to confess, there was a time that I would not have had much to write down. I worked hard and reacted to the demands of the day, but if something had happened to me and I had wanted to leave my children a book of "wisdom" or even a videotape of my philosophy, I would have had embarrassingly little to convey. I can honestly say that this book, *Life Code: The New Rules for Winning in the Real World*, goes a long way toward filling that void. There would be more that came from me personally, but whatever I conveyed would include what is written here, especially this chapter.

I would want them, and I want you to know, that I believe we can create moments in time in which all things wrong can be made right. I have done it, I have seen others do it, and I believe you can and will do it too. When you get to that precipice, that critical moment in time, you have to be ready, as in spring-loaded ready, to seize the moment and be there with purpose toward a well-defined goal. I have often said winners do things losers do not want to do, and I am ready to tell you what those things are. To be candid, this new "Life Code" playbook will likely take you out of your comfort zone. It may also add to, modify, or contradict a lot of what you have been taught. Maybe it will inspire you to require more from yourself, or maybe it will simply give you permission to be more aggressive in the pursuit of life quality, but either way, it is designed to create a difference in your life. You may find that parts of this code of winning conduct seem to parallel some of the "Nefarious 15" in the bad guys' playbook. Not everything they do to exploit and take unfair advantage is, in and of itself, wrong-headed. Some of their tactics become nefarious only in their application and intent. Some of what they do is done simply because it works. Just because they abuse that power does not mean you should be denied access to those tools any more than the police should be denied the use of firearms just because violent criminals *misuse* them. So, here is your "Life Code" playbook with what I call the "Sweet 16" important strategies, mind-sets, tactics, and behaviors to create more of what you want in your life.

The "Life Code" Playbook

#1: You must have a defined "image" and never go out of character.

It's not enough just to *know* yourself. You also need to know how to *present* yourself. I made this the number-one point in your playbook because it is critically important and potentially outcome-determinative. You have to decide how you're going to project yourself to the world. Once you do, you must commit to it 100 percent. You can't ride two horses at the same time, so deciding on your image, your personal definition, is so important. It is the horse you'll ride through your future life. Please understand, I'm not asking you to be phony and wear a mask.

Quite the contrary. I think it is important that your image, the image you consciously decide to project to other people, is authentic and congruent with who you really are.

Everybody—including you and me—presents their image in a way that makes a statement, a statement about who they are. You obviously have to be very mindful of that statement, that image, every time you step out, especially into the competitive world, because it sets an important tone for all that happens in your world.

Understand that you have always made a statement. Just because you may not have intended to or strategically selected and refined it doesn't mean you don't still project it. Maybe you've been passive about it, and if so, it's time to get very active and consciously immerse yourself in both the process and the end product. To embrace this playbook and the strategy associated with it, you simply can't be passive any longer. There is no reality, only perception. You will be judged and reacted to by who people "believe" you to be, not necessarily who you *are*. Again, that does not make you a phony, but it can make you successful. I cannot state this strongly enough because it is the lynchpin to so much of how the world and everybody in it reacts to you.

You cannot define yourself one way and then do a "180" and expect to be successful in love, business, society, or anywhere else.

Think about great leaders of our time, for example, Winston Churchill and Gen. George S. Patton. They both, at times, must have been scared half to death wondering where the will or the way to victory would come from. But do you think they got in front of the world media or their countrymen or troops and displayed fear and anxiety? Absolutely not, and that did not mean they were phony. They had an image of "never say die" invincibility, and they never, ever "broke character." Neither should you, not ever. That means in all areas of your life. For example, do not, I repeat, *do not*, expect people to take you seriously and then turn around on a Saturday night and get stupid on Facebook or YouTube or other social platforms by posting pictures or comments you do not want read back to you in a job interview or by your future father-in-law or from the newspaper tomorrow morning. You cannot define yourself one way and then do a "180" and expect to be successful in love, business, society, or anywhere else. And please realize (and tell your children because they have the *knowledge* to use the Internet but not the *wisdom*) that once something gets onto the Internet, it is there *forever*! The same is true for emails. Never, ever put sensitive content, content that can be taken out of context, in writing, especially in an email. Instead, pick up the phone or go in person and have a real conversation.

I've always said, "If you're in a hole, then **stop digging!***"*

Reputation is critically important, so consciously define and protect it at every turn. You may have a hard time undoing damage you may have already done, but you can sure stop yourself from continuing to hurt yourself from this moment forward by making more intelligent choices. I've always said, "If you're in a hole, then *stop digging*!" So get active about it and ask yourself *what* statement you're making and if it is the statement you want to make and if that statement is authentic to who you really are. A great "test" of your statement is to ask yourself, or even someone else, what people say about you when you're not around, in other words, what they say behind your back. If you can get honest feedback from yourself or others, it can be very instructive. I think it's very important for people to *own* the statement they make. If your statement is that you are hard-edged, no-nonsense, and a tough, goal-oriented taskmaster, then you have to own that and not complain if people don't relate or refer to you as "warm and fuzzy." You can't make that kind of statement and then be upset when people respond to you in kind.

You might make somewhat different statements in various settings because you are not a one-dimensional, one-trick pony. But even those differing statements should be authentic and consistent with your chosen projected image. For example, as a woman, you might have a business persona that reflects your commitment and seriousness. But when you're in a dating or romantic setting, you might find that persona simply doesn't work for you because it can be intimidating to men. So, in a romantic situation, you may want to rotate other authentic characteristics to the forefront. It is still *you*, still consistent with your image, but is a different *part* of who you are.

I wrote a book a few years back entitled *Love Smart*, with a chapter dealing with what I called "The Character of You." This is the broad and all-encompassing definition of who you are from the inside out. It underlies what I call a "defined product," which is whatever side you choose to exhibit in a given situation. The first person you need to sell yourself to is you because once you accept this authentic character—with all your skills, traits, abilities, and characteristics—then you can commit to it, maximize it, embrace it, and love it. As I said, you absolutely must commit to this "lock, stock, and barrel" because this is the horse you're going to ride. Commit to it, own it, love it, and live it. Anything less is a loser for sure. You teach people how to treat you. If you want to be treated with dignity and respect, then you must carry yourself with dignity and respect. If you want to be treated like a diva, then you must act like a diva, with your head always held high.

Once you have identified your strengths and defined and committed to the image and statement that you are projecting, a sense of peace and power is going to come over you. Once that occurs, and it can, you need to be very sensitive to it and play to your audience.

Does this newfound power, calmness, and presence have the effect of intimidating or putting off other people? If so, be sensitive to that. The really smooth, audience-sensitive player knows when to dial it up and when to dial it down. I know people who are so good at what they do that they just never make a mistake. I have even seen these people intentionally "screw up" or make "choreographed mistakes," just to seem human. I have seen them use self-effacing humor to make themselves more approachable and less intimidating.

You teach people how to treat you.

You want to do what works. It does you no good to complete this homework and get completely comfortable with yourself if you then go project an image that puts other people off or makes them uncomfortable. What you want is results, and if that means you need to humanize yourself to avoid a perception of being "perfect," then so be it.

Approach this as though you were creating a character in a movie or a play. How would you describe the character? What would be the appearance? Wardrobe? Weight? Beliefs? Behaviors? Personality? Sense of humor? Hobbies? Activities? Energy level? And on and on. This really should be fun if you do it with the right attitude. Remember, you're the star in the script of your own life, so act like it by embracing your authentic self! Create it and then commit to it.

#2: You must create a perception of uniqueness.

When I say you need to be "unique," I mean that you need to choose to define the image we just discussed such that you distinguish yourself from anyone else in this world. We have enough sheep; we have enough cattle that just belong to the herd and blend into the background. If you want to be a winner, you need to find, embrace, and project those things that set you apart from everyone else. Uniqueness is valuable in so many different respects. I very much believe in a defined product. I think people need to know what they get when they get you. I have subscribed to this philosophy my entire life, including right now, as I'm writing this book.

Remember, you're the star in the script of
your own life, so act like it by embracing your
authentic self!

Think about it, when someone says to you, "Dr. Phil," what comes to mind? You may like me, you may love me, or you may watch me and think some village must be missing its idiot! But, wherever you come down on "Dr. Phil," I'm betting you won't confuse me with anybody else. You may think I am a barbarian or a bastion of much-needed common sense, but I'll tell you what—you're not going to mistake me for someone else, and you probably won't be indifferent. I have always strived to be unique, long before I was ever on television, and I think that's a good thing. Even being bald can be a distinguishing factor! I live in Hollywood, and I don't know many people on television who look like me. (Thank God for small favors.) I have a friend who always tells me, "Doc, you have a great face for radio!" And you know what? He's probably right! I may not be the best-looking guy on TV, but I am unique. You should be too.

It doesn't always take some huge thing to distinguish yourself from the herd. I have a good friend in Texas who is a big-time, heavy-hitting litigator. He's constantly in trial, locked in vicious combat with the other side. But in contrast to that hostile back-drop, he goes out of his way to make a show of being a gracious Southern gentleman before, during, and after the contest, as though he were Rhett Butler with a law degree. It distinguishes him and it works for him because, while he may play it out very consciously, it is still totally authentic. He distinguishes himself by creating a sharp contrast to the context in which he exists. What does that say about our world when you can successfully distinguish yourself from the masses simply by showing manners? The point is, it can be something big, small, or a compilation of small things that set you apart and make you memorable to others.

If, in fact, you don't feel like you are unique, then it may be time to *reinvent* yourself. You can do so without abandoning who you are because we all have a *range* of traits, skills, abilities, and the capability to move about within that range. Reinvention may mean changing everything from your look to what you do, where you do it, or the way you engage people. It may mean changing your focus or the goals you seek to attain. It may mean building on what you like best about yourself. It is a conscious project about you and can be very stimulating. At *Dr. Phil*, we finish our season each year at the end of May. I always wait a few weeks to let everyone take a deep breath and decompress, and then we begin to meet and strategize about the upcoming fall season. We spend every summer reinventing ourselves. We challenge ourselves to figure how we can do a better job of telling our stories and getting our message out. This has led to a number of innovations that have plowed new ground in the world of television. We created the "Dr. Phil House" where we actually bring families in distress to us so we can study and work with them on camera. We developed a procedure for installing motion-activated cameras in people's actual homes so we could observe patterns of interaction between parents and children over several weeks in their home environment, which might contain important triggers for certain behaviors. We created home video–diary cameras so future guests can record themselves at critical and often highly instructive times in their life, even if it is 3 a.m. We built all of these innovations and integrated them into who we have defined ourselves to be. By the way, reinventing yourself can be really refreshing.

If, in fact, you don't feel like you are unique, then it may be time to reinvent yourself.

#3: You must play "big," not just long.

In this day and time, it's simply not enough to keep your head down, work hard, put in your time, and expect a reward at the end because that "end" may never arrive. Playing *big* is dramatically different from playing *long*, because plodders, even reliable and competent ones, seldom win big. Sometimes they don't win at all. This is not a pleasant message to deliver, but it's one you need to hear. Current events have shown us that a lot of long-term employees are the first to go when corporations cut back. Seniority means nothing when performance is what's critical to a company's survival. How many stories have you heard about folks who have put in years of faithful service only to be turned out just short of qualifying for retirement? Longevity may have meant something once, but I'm just not sure it does anymore. There was a time that if you wanted to describe something as being a sure bet, you might say, "You can take *that* to the bank." Times have changed, and there isn't a lot that seems stable in the long-run anymore, least of all banks! It may mean that you need to exercise more urgency in your pursuits than in times gone by. Residing low profile smack in the middle of the pack is no longer a safe way to go through life.

There is a new "Life Code" in today's world that calls for different strategies, and if you want to win big, you have to play big, now.

That means you're going to have to rethink a lot of things you may have believed since your childhood. A lot of beliefs instilled by your role models and other trusted, well-meaning people— your parents, your teachers, and your friends, whose advice and behavior you have relied on—may not be relevant in today's highly competitive and less predictable environment. Remember, we teach people how to treat us. There is a new "Life Code" in today's world that calls for different strategies, and if you want to win big, you have to play big, now.

You need to *get* attention, not avoid it. You need to do things that put you on the radar, and you do that by making noise, by playing big. We use a lot of experts on our shows, *The Doctors* and *Dr. Phil.* We might send a film crew to San Francisco to interview some world-class expert and spend five hours taping him as he does what he does in his office. When he finally watches the show and sees his segment, it might last a minute and 18 seconds. He says, "Wow! You were at my place for five hours, and you used only a minute and 18 seconds? Did I do poorly?" No! You did just fine, but you're measuring with the wrong yardstick. You want to play it big, not long. I would rather have a memorable minute and 18 seconds than bore the audience for 20 minutes. I've never heard a viewer say, "Wow! Did you see how long that guy was on *Dr. Phil* yesterday?" but I have heard them say, "Wow, that expert on Dr. Phil yesterday changed the way I think! He had a huge impact on me!" Make an impact—that's the test. In fact, I have a rule for *Dr. Phil*: If a tape takes longer than about a minute and 30 seconds to tell the story, we probably need to get a new guest or a new expert or a new something, because if you can't make an impact in less time than that, you've got the wrong cat on camera. In television, a minute and a half is an eternity.

In the same way, when it's your turn in the spotlight, at home, at work, or in a social setting, and you want to establish yourself in a strong way and play it big, you need to be the one who makes an impression. When they leave and go home or when they're at lunch tomorrow, you want them to be buzzing about what you said, what you did, or how you looked. You want to make an impression, one that people remember. You have to make noise; you have to rise above everybody else's noise and become the *figure* that pops from the *background* of everybody else.

You have to stand out in some positive, constructive way. Some people you know just naturally get that. They may dress a little flamboyantly when at the office, just to get attention. Or, to take another example, management might be doing a new layout at the office, and you may say, "I don't really care where my desk is. Does anybody really care?" You *better believe* somebody else does. Somebody is going to say, "I'd like to be right here. I'll just take this desk." And you know what? That desk just might be positioned such that it and whoever is sitting there are the first things the boss sees when she arrives in the morning and the last things she sees when she leaves at night. Out of everybody on the staff, that person sitting at that desk has the most frequent exposure to the power structure of the office. And while your co-worker stepped up and claimed that spot, you were openly saying, "I don't care, put me behind the potted planted over there." But if the boss doesn't see you doing your work, she may very well not appreciate it or acknowledge you for doing it.

Like it or not, I'm telling you the truth. If playing big feels contrary to your personality, if it is out of your comfort zone, keep in mind that you can do it in your own way—the bottom line is that you need to do it. Playing it big isn't just about being *loud*. It comes down to either you doing what I am describing or you just being another face in the crowd and hoping that when they come to "thin the herd," you're not on that faceless hit list.

#4: Learn to claim and accept praise, and acknowledge it in a gracious way, but *do* accept it.

A main tenet of the new "Life Code" is this: There is absolutely, unequivocally, no way that you are going to win in this world without being noticed, accepted, admired, complimented, sought after, and appreciated. Every strategy you embrace and every action plan you execute should be designed to distinguish you in a positive way. That's why I began detailing this part of the new "Life Code" by telling you that you must create and adhere to a unique goal. The goal is to get noticed *and* acknowledged for who you are and what you do. That's true across the board—in your career, within your family, in your social circles, and in your romantic relationships. Being acknowledged for positive traits, qualities, values, behaviors, skills, and abilities is a good thing! If it isn't happening for you now and you want to be successful, then you need to change what you are doing.

A main tenet of the new "Life Code" is this:
There is absolutely, unequivocally, no way
that you are going to win in this world without
being noticed, accepted, admired, complimented,
sought after, and appreciated.

Why do most people get so very uncomfortable when they actually *achieve* that acknowledgment? I suppose people think it shows humility to give an "Aw, shucks, it weren't nothing!" response as they dig their toe in the carpet and blush.

I don't get that. If you work your butt off to get ahead or be accepted, loved, acknowledged, or admired and then someone who can actually open that door for you finally takes notice and even compliments you, why wouldn't you graciously accept the compliment or the invitation to move to that next level? I can think of only two reasons: You've been taught it is prideful and narcissistic to seek attention, so you shun it when it comes, or you do not believe you really deserve the praise.

Let me remove that first obstacle right now. It is not prideful or egotistical to accept, claim, or expect praise. You need to choose to respond differently when someone praises you or confirms your value. In fact, you should work out your response in advance and rehearse giving it so you don't choke under pressure and revert to your old, outdated response pattern. How about simply learning and practicing to say,

"Thank you for saying that, you are kind to notice." Or,

"That means so much coming from you, so thank you for noticing and saying so." Or,

"Thank you so much; I have worked very hard and have had a lot of help, so thank you from all of us. With your permission, I will pass your kind words on to my team or co-workers."

If it is in a personal or romantic situation that you are comfortable with, you can reciprocate at the level of the comment you received. It is always safe to begin with a very straightforward "Thank you for your kind words" and add any specific reaction to what was said.

As for the second obstacle, if you don't believe you deserve the credit, the praise, or the acknowledgment, then others will soon follow your cue in thinking you don't deserve it. I, for one, believe people most likely know themselves a lot better than I do, and if *they* think they're undeserving, then who am I to question them? If I praise someone and they pooh-pooh it, then okay—maybe they are right, and I was wrong! But you shouldn't want to convince your would-be "fans" that their confidence in you is misplaced. If your "personal truth" is so damaged that you can't even accept a compliment, then you are your own biggest obstacle, and repairing that should go on the top of your "to-do" list.

#5: You must become "essential."

In addition to embracing your best image, being unique, and getting noticed by playing big, you also need to become *essential*.

Common sense should make this point pretty self-explanatory. If you want to succeed in any situation—personal, professional, romantic, social, or familial—it's important to be needed. It is good to be relied upon. It is good to be essential.

We have been in tough economic times for a number of years now. Businesses have been downsizing and eliminating people who are, in most instances, quite capable. But I'll tell you who did not get eliminated—the people who wore a lot of different hats, could be relied on to do multiple tasks, or had specialized information or knowledge about the business. People who knew what to do when the air conditioner didn't work or how to get the computers back online when the temperamental router got overheated—these people are not good candidates for downsizing. People who have become the trusted contact person for the company's clientele or have become essential to the formal or informal running of the business tend to survive as well. Employees whom the boss has come to rely upon to make his or her life easier are obviously in a great spot. Those people are all essential and difficult to replace. Endeavor to be one of those people.

The same is true in a social situation or a romantic situation. If you come to be the go-to person within a group or if you are perceived to be a critically important support system, you are not likely to be eliminated. In a romantic relationship, if you "complete" him, as Tom Cruise so famously said of Renée Zellweger in the movie *Jerry Maguire*, you'll be sticking around.

You may be thinking, "Dr. Phil, are you telling me to create some kind of codependency or invite unhealthy reliance from others?" Sort of, except for the codependency and unhealthy part. What I'm telling you is to become an essential, vital player in whatever situation or scenario you are in. "Codependency" is a clinical term that doesn't even apply here. Common sense tells you that if they don't miss you when you're gone, chances are pretty good you are going to be just that—gone. I don't want you to just hope this doesn't happen to you; I want you to find actions you can take toward becoming an essential, irreplaceable element in any situation or scenario that you value. This should become a conscious priority—a mission.

What I'm telling you is to become an essential, vital player in whatever situation or scenario you are in.

And while we're talking about common sense, you want to guard and protect what you know. Do *not* give away the recipe to the "secret sauce." Remember there is no reality, only perception, so maintain at least the perception of being irreplaceable. If you're out there flapping your mouth about your unique knowledge, it's no longer unique! Don't teach ten people information that makes you much less unique and essential. You don't want to dilute your value. If people believe that they can't get by without you, that is a good thing in this competitive world.

#6: You must know your *real* currency.

If you haven't had an honest conversation with yourself about what you *really* want, you can spend years getting to an end result that simply won't do it for you. Don't waste valuable time working for what you *don't* want. The saying "Different strokes for different folks" applies here. Some people strive for a promotion because they need the money, while others seek the acknowledgment. Neither is right or wrong, just different. The key is to not waste time or effort even on short-term goals if they cannot yield what you really want and need; it's simply inefficient. The key is knowing your *real* currency, or else you inadvertently spend time doing things that, even if they go 100 percent perfectly, cannot and will not generate what you want. Don't spend even five minutes doing things that simply can't get you what you want.

For example, I have a personal rule when dealing with any organization, agency, or group. This may sound minor at first, but if you think about it, this is anything but a minor strategy. If I am trying to get some person or organization to do something for me, I absolutely will not talk to anyone who *can't* say yes. There might be three layers of customer service personnel who cannot depart from policy. They may want to, they may be blown away by my persuasiveness and logic, *but* they are authorized only to say "no." So, if what I want is "yes," why would I spend even one minute talking to someone who can say only "no"? I wouldn't, and neither should you. I want to rely on me to get it done, so I don't want to tell them and then they go tell the decision maker. No thanks! I'll plead my own case; I'll put my money on me.

There are many different kinds of "currency." Be attuned to all the different ways you can be rewarded in a given situation. We all know about monetary currency, but there is also mental, emotional, social, security, and spiritual currency. Maybe the guy you're in a relationship with won't ask you to marry him right away, but raising the issue helps you achieve some clarity that gives you peace of mind and creates a timetable you can live with. That's currency. Maybe you don't immediately get the manager's job, but you do get a raise, and you are now on the boss's radar as someone looking to move up. That's monetary and social currency. Pay attention to all of the ways that you can get paid off. Either way, define what you really want, and do not invest in people or situations that couldn't give it to you even if they wanted to.

#7: **You must always, always have a plan.**

Being spontaneous is great if you want to show your fun-loving side or your spirit of adventure on a date or out with some friends. But if you want to achieve a sustained measure of success in any area of your life, *you need a plan.* You need a very specific plan—a plan that begins with identifying what it is that you want.

Sounds simple, right? But only a surprisingly small percentage of people can actually tell you how they define success. That ability puts those people at a distinct advantage because they can tell you exactly what they want and describe it in great detail and in measurable terms so they know when they have arrived.

Declarations like "I want to be happy" just don't cut it. You want to be happy? My dog wants to be happy. But the real question is what happiness is *for you*. If you say "peace in my life," then I would ask you to define "peace." It's all about specificity. Don't be an "unguided missile." Create a guidance system for yourself by first determining exactly where you are and precisely where you want to be, and then identify the action steps necessary to get there. The difference between a goal and a dream is a timeline and an action plan. If you want to be the manager at your place of employment, then you need to come up with a plan that will get you from the job you're in now to any job that is a stepping-stone to the manager's job and then to the manager's job. Just wanting it won't make it happen, but targeting it with an action plan will. You should get up every single day with a purpose in mind. "Today I will achieve this specific thing, with this intended result." Anything less, and you're just floating along like a leaf in a stream. Power up! Take specific action toward a known outcome every single day of your life.

I would give you the same advice if your goal, instead of a managerial job, was to get your heartthrob to pop the question, walk down the aisle, and marry you. Your action plan might include such things as figuring out what's holding him back and then coming up with a solution to overcome his paralysis. If his parents got an ugly divorce and therefore he is scared of merging his life with yours, then you need to acknowledge that and then come up with *a plan* to alleviate his fears. Just going on date after date or moving in together does not target the goal.

Take specific action toward a known outcome every single day of your life.

You must have plans that do not let days turn into weeks, weeks into months, and months into years, as you sit on the porch and watch your life pass by. Make a plan and write it down with great specificity. Doing it in your head just isn't effective. You need to write it out so you can refer to it later. Don't just read right over this and then do it haphazardly in your head (that's what I would be tempted to do). There is such power in the objectivity you will gain by writing it out and seeing it in black and white.

SEVEN KEY STRATEGIES FOR ATTAINING YOUR GOAL

This is based on a list I have espoused since the 1990s when I wrote about it in *Life Strategies.* Use it as a way to clearly define your goal, a timeline, and the steps necessary for achieving it. For more details on these strategies, go to DrPhil.com.

#1: Express your goal in terms of specific events or behaviors. (For example, "my goal is to actively return to college in a degree program.")

I want: _____

_____

_____

#2: Express your goal in terms that can be measured. (Take six hours per night school or online semester until degree secured.)

Specifically, that means: _____

_____

_____

#3: Assign a timeline to your goal. (Complete six hours by next May. Degree by end of sixth semester.)

My realistic timeline is: _____

_____

_____

SEVEN KEY STRATEGIES FOR
ATTAINING YOUR GOAL *(continued)*

#4: Choose a goal you can control. (Attending college works here.)

The circumstances I can control in achieving this goal are: _____

_____

_____

#5: Plan and program a strategy that will get you to your goal. (Make sure you have the money, time, and access. Set up schedule realistically.)

Potential obstacles are: _____

_____

_____

Resources required are: _____

_____

_____

#6: Define your goal in terms of steps. (Choose a school, apply for admission, select your courses, and so on.)

The necessary steps are: _____

_____

_____

SEVEN KEY STRATEGIES FOR
ATTAINING YOUR GOAL *(continued)*

#7: Create accountability for your progress toward your goal: ("My sister will call me once a week to make sure I've taken steps in the past seven days toward obtaining my college degree.")

I will create accountability by: _____

_____

_____

_____

We're not finished yet, though. Now write the answer to this imperative question:

How will you feel when you obtain your goal? _____

_____

_____

_____

Take special note of #7 on the list. Now that you have defined the goal and the action plan for achieving it in great detail, you will be so much more efficient than those around you that suddenly it's going to look like they're moving in reverse! Since you now have a plan in place, the next step is to set up some type of external accountability system with a trusted person in your life. Face them every Friday, for example, to see whether you achieved the week's interim steps toward your ultimate goal. This will help you stay on target.

#8: You must keep things "close to the vest."

You never want to be predictable. You know that from your time in the dating world, right? The worst thing you can do is to allow yourself to be taken for granted, to be a "sure thing." To be interesting is to be powerful. And to be interesting, you have to maintain a certain degree of mystery, because it gives you a degree of mastery. Mystery draws people to you because they are curious who you are and how you do what you do. They will check to see where you stand on an issue and see what you think is important. They will check because you are not predictable, so they must. The old saying "Familiarity breeds contempt" is all too often true. Cardinal Richelieu said it well: "If you give me six lines written by the hand of the most honest of men, I will find something in them which will hang him." The message is clear: Limit your words. People tend to "over-share." My dad always said, "Boy, don't ever miss a good chance to *shut up*!" Good advice.

If your "friends" and co-workers don't know what you are after, they are less likely to get in your way. Never let them see you "making sausage." While you are in the planning stages, be discreet, very discreet. It is critically important that you realize that so many aspects of your life are in fact competitive. There may be some people in your life you sit around the fire and sing "Kumbaya" with, but I'm betting it's fewer than you might think. And there is often competition even within a unit or team. I played team sports all my life, and when we suited up and went onto the field to play the opposing team, we were one for all and all for one. But the other six days a week we were jockeying for position. We were fighting for that first-string, starting role on the team. We might have 90 guys on the football team, but only 11 of us were going to walk on that field when the whistle blew.

We all wanted to be among those 11, and that made for a lot of competition.

Competition is certainly not a bad thing, especially if you are good at it. Competition pushes you, it makes you better, and it makes you tougher. But no matter how you feel about competition, do not kid yourself—that is exactly what your life is all about. Unless you've got the crummiest job on the globe, I promise you there is somebody who is ready and willing to take it away from you, if you don't protect it. Unless you're married to the lousiest husband or wife in the world (and maybe even if you are), there is somebody out there who would be more than happy to take him or her away from you.

> *And to be interesting, you have to maintain a certain degree of mystery, because it gives you a degree of mastery.*

We don't live in a socialist society—and there is definitely a hierarchy, a pecking order, if you will, where most people are vying to improve their position and improve their life. Now, you may not like that, you may think it's beneath you, and that's okay. It's okay for you think it's vulgar, but that won't change anything for you. There's always some old guy or girl spring-loaded to pop up and "eat your sack lunch" if you don't stay alert and sharp and have a private plan discreetly pursued. Seriously, if you share with your co-worker that a job opportunity has opened up at another company that pays more money with better benefits and she applies for it and beats you out, you are going to wish you had "zipped it up" at your current job and kept your plans close to the vest!

When Dallas gets ready to play New York in the NFL, I can promise you with 100 percent certainty that the Cowboys do not send their playbook and specific game plan to the Giants with a note that says, "We didn't want to catch you guys by surprise, so here is our playbook and game plan for this coming Sunday. We hope this helps us have a better bonding experience on the field. Signed, the Dallas Cowboys." They don't do it, and neither should you. If you're paying attention to what I'm saying, you are going to have a plan, but make it a discreet plan. Don't tell people what it is that you want, and certainly don't tell them how you plan to go about getting it unless they have earned your utmost trust and confidence. If you tell Suzy Q that you're really interested in marrying ol' Dave over there, she just might be thinking, "Well, I never really paid much attention to ol' Dave, but now that she mentioned it, now that she's interested in him, maybe I've missed something. I think I just might take another look."

If you think this sounds really paranoid and pessimistic, you're wrong. It's just human nature. Keep your plan private, and guard it jealously. The same goes with any other relevant information that you have in any competitive situation. Even though it doesn't have to do with the overall plan, I can assure you that the Dallas Cowboys also did not send the New York Giants a detailed list of their injuries or the players they thought were just really not up to par. Nor should you let your competitors know what's going on in your life that might be draining your energy or making demands on your time, particularly when you run into the kind of BAITERs I've been describing in this book. They will use that like ammunition for a gun.

#9: You must always be in investigatory mode.

If you accept my premise that the vast majority of your life is competitive, then it makes perfect sense that you should always pay attention to what's going on around you. But I want you to do more than just pay attention. I want you to proactively be in constant investigatory mode, constantly gathering relevant information that may empower you to do and achieve that which you desire. It's long been said that "knowledge is power," and nothing could be truer. That is exactly why BAITERs are always building an arsenal of information. They do it to *misuse* it; you will do it to *use* it. This is exactly why I told you to always play it close to the vest. I want the *power to be yours* to use in a competitive situation, not theirs to use against you in a competitive situation.

---

*I'm suggesting here that you
become a private detective who is
"psychologically-minded."*

Become a student of human nature. Seriously, I want you to start thinking about the psychology of the situation, the agendas, and the motivations of the players. Become a student of everything that is in play in any given situation. Pay attention to how relevant people react to different happenings, events, or stimuli. What sets them off? What embarrasses them? What angers them? What intimidates them? What are the alliances and allegiances within the group that you're involved with? What motivates different people to do what they do? I promise you that not everyone in your work group or social group is motivated by, or in pursuit of, the same things. Common sense tells you that if you pay attention to who hangs out with whom, that can be valuable information if somebody comes at you at some point. What can you learn about someone's background? Often this information can be both diagnostic of the current situation and predictive of the future.

It's also important to remember that only 7 percent of all communication is verbal. The other 93 percent is nonverbal— including body language, facial expression, eye contact, syntax, tone—and environmental. By environmental, I simply mean the circumstances of somebody saying something of relevance— where were they when they said it and who was around at the time it was said. That might inform you greatly as to their motive behind the comment.

I'm suggesting here that you become a private detective who is "psychologically-minded." By "psychologically-minded" I mean you should pay attention to the fact that statements and behaviors often occur for other than the apparent reasons. Most often, those "other reasons" come from the inside out. They are motivated by emotion, and to understand the statement or the actions fully, how to deal with the person who's making them, or how to get that person to do what you want, you need to consider what is driving them to say and do the things they do. This will give you a tremendous leg up on the competition—if you're coming in with a plan, a private plan, you are extremely goal-oriented, and you are not the least bit in denial about the fact that life is a full-contact competition. If you embrace all these things, you should never, ever be caught asleep at the switch. This takes energy, it's true, but either you are in it to win it or you aren't. You are worth the effort, and it's high time you stepped up for the mate, job, change, or peace of mind that you want.

#10: You must "stretch" and behave your way to success, even if it feels like "fake it until you make it."

Let me be clear right up front, I am *not* advocating that you go through life as a fraud. What I am telling you is that if you get an opportunity to move to the next level in your job, for example, do not—repeat *do not*—listen to self-doubt and take yourself out because you don't think you know everything you need to know in order to do what you think you're going to be asked to do.

The moment that opportunity knocks is not the time to be overcome with humility, self-effacement, and self-doubt. Some people might call this "fake it till you make it." Others might say that winners "behave their way to success." Of course, you have to use reasonable judgment here. If people's lives and well-being hang in the balance, you're in a different situation than if somebody wants you to take over the sales department at your company. I'm not advocating that you get all macho about your ability to do brain surgery if, in fact, you're a nurse or technician, any more than the surgeon could do your job. What I'm saying is you need to have confidence and be bold enough to stretch yourself, scramble to close the gap if one exists, and grow into new opportunities.

If having mastery of a skill set and successful experience were required for being parents, there would be millions and millions of orphans in this world, including my children. But you know what? People do it every day. They figure it out as they go along. They have confidence enough in themselves to be adaptive, surround themselves with competent people, and get the job done.

Whether it's "fake it till you make it" or "behave your way to success," you have to give yourself a chance to play at the next level. That takes confidence and a willingness to stretch and take a risk. And by all means, once you take the leap, then become a ravenous consumer of every bit of information you can find. It doesn't matter whether it's from a book, a magazine, a news article, or some blog that you find on the Internet. Information is information; look under every rock to find something that informs you about the task at hand. Do not sit around passively waiting for somebody to send you to a class or take you by the hand and walk you through what it is you're going to have to do. Take the initiative and grab information at every turn. And work smart, not just hard. Use the resources at your fingertips. Delegate to people who, although they may not see the big managerial picture, they probably have enough knowledge of the parts and pieces necessary to succeed. Delegation also allows you to multiply your power and yet stay in control. Be the portal for information with your bosses, but let others do as much as possible.

What I'm saying is you need to have confidence and be bold enough to stretch yourself, scramble to close the gap if one exists, and grow into new opportunities.

It's been said that "good judgment comes from experience, and experience comes from really bad judgment." So, get some experience! And by the way, there's a really good chance that the other people involved in the situation don't know one bit more about it than you do. Give yourself a chance to succeed, whether it is in your love life or professional life or whatever. Take your shot. A risk-free life can be really boring, and the clock is ticking. Don't let life pass you by because you're playing it safe and sitting on the sidelines. The world is moving at a faster and faster rate, and it's becoming easier and easier to fall behind in your own life. The new "Life Code" calls for playing big and playing bold. I promise that at the end of your life, it will not be the times you said "no" along the way that you will look back on fondly and with pride. Taking reasonable risks is not reckless, and if it is the potential of failure or embarrassment that frightens you, remember that you now know how to play the "what if?" game all the way to the end.

#11: You must always keep your options open.

I do not believe in management by ultimatums, and I don't believe in embracing rigid positions that take away your ability to move and adapt. For example, I don't believe in going "nuclear" with kids, saying things like, "If I catch you drinking, you are grounded for life and will never get your driver's license!" Now, I might agree with that sentiment, but my problems are with "life" and "never." It leaves you nowhere to go; you have closed off your options. What do you do once you have grounded your child for life and told them that they will never drive an automobile? What are you going to do next, chain them in a dungeon?

Always leave yourself a face-saving way out. As we say in Texas, when you "throw down the hoe handle," there's nothing left to do but fight. Threats and ultimatums—particularly involving extreme consequences—paint you into a corner and leave you nowhere to go. Plus, particularly at work or in a relationship, you would be disclosing too much about what you think and feel. If you tell your boss, "If you hire her, I quit!" or if you tell your significant other, "If your crazy sister moves in with you, I am out of here!" then you're trapped. There's no way you can change your position without losing face. If in fact you believe that you'll be looking for the door if the boss hires some-body you think is bad news or if your significant other's crazy sister moves in, that's okay—but why say so? The only possible reason would be to try to manipulate someone into not doing something they intend to do. But there are a whole lot better ways to dissuade them than painting yourself into a corner. If you're going to leave, you don't need to telegraph it. And if you're not going to, then don't say you are—because if your bluff gets called, you wind up looking like a wuss.

Once you declare your position, your leverage is
gone, and winners never give up their leverage.

So, keep your options open, and don't tell people everything you're thinking. I can name 100 people who would be shocked to know how I really feel about them. They don't know because they don't need to know, and I don't need them to know. If it's nothing more than leverage and manipulation that you are look-ing for, go at it in a way that doesn't paint you into a corner.

If there is a power struggle going on and you feel pressured and paint yourself into a corner, I promise you have just been manipulated by one side or the other, as they were trying to build an alliance. Once you declare your position, your leverage is gone, and winners never give up their leverage.

#12: You must always master the system and figure a way to make it work for you.

Whatever situation or circumstance you find yourself in will have rules, parameters, and almost always subtle nuances. And I'm not just talking about formal structures; there is always a dynamic that defines the give-and-take of life. You can gain a distinct advantage if you know, and I mean really know, the game better than anybody else.

When I started my doctoral training program, I had heard that it was one of the best programs in the country but that it was notoriously slow in terms of actually getting graduates out the door. Apparently they, like many complex academic programs, had a reputation for "moving the finish line" by changing requirements every time there was a change of leadership, and students wound up caught in the crossfire. So, when I arrived, rather than just diving right into my academic work, I studied the system to figure out whether there were ways that I could avoid having such a long journey in pursuit of a "moving target." I dug deep and wide, and what I learned was that at some point during your matriculation, you were to file a "degree plan," which is a *contract* between you and the university setting out exactly what will be required of you before you are awarded your degree. That set of requirements is governed by what is listed in the university catalog in force *at the time you file your plan.* Most students are in no hurry to get a degree plan filed because they expect to be there for at least five years, and it is a time-consuming process, so what's the hurry? I didn't wait; I completed and filed mine in the first week.

The point is obvious: If you know the system, the game, and you really know how it's played, you have a distinct advantage over your competition.

Fast-forward four years down the road when it was time for me to leave for my internship. I had completed all of the requirements outlined in my signed degree plan when the administration informed me that I in fact had another full year of requirements to complete—requirements that had been added a little at a time over the last several years. Wrong! I whipped out my *filed and signed* degree plan (*a contract*) that said if I completed the requirements outlined in the catalog at the time of filing that I was to be awarded my diploma. The additional year's worth of requirements did not apply to me but applied to everyone who had not studied the system and filed their degree plan in a timely fashion. I studied the system, and I made it work for me. I also understood why the average course of academics was seven years when it should have been four or five.

The point is obvious: If you know the system, you know the game, and you really know how it's played, so you have a distinct advantage over your competition. And make no mistake about it, you're in a game, whether you like it or not. It's up to you how well you play it—or whether you get played. Know the rules, know your options, and know how to use the system to your advantage. Like so much of the new "Life Code," what I'm advocating here takes effort, but it will pay off in spades.

#13: You must create a passionate nucleus of supporters.

Winners are not lone rangers. You should strive to surround yourself with a nucleus of people who share your passion, share your vision, and support your pursuit of your goals. It is important to understand that people do not bond head-to-head; they bond heart-to-heart. Your goal is to get your nucleus of supporters to buy into your agenda not just intellectually but emotionally. This is a hugely important piece of information.

Also, recognize the reality that *everyone* approaches *every* situation at least in part asking the question, "What is in this for me?" If you can answer that question for your potential supporters, they are much more likely to truly get behind you.

You can create this emotional buy-in by empathetically putting yourself in the position of your potential supporters and seeing things through their eyes. You will need to figure out how to make it clear to those people how your success is in their best interest and that of the team. You cannot be at all places all the time; you cannot cover every demand or contingency by yourself. You need a team, and you need that team to be emotionally motivated toward a common goal. The team must see that you are "their guy." They must see that you will lead them, protect them, and advocate for them. When they see this, they will do amazing things to ensure your success. We have talked about "playing big," and you need to play big on their behalf. They need to see you advocating for them; they need to see you doing things that help them in their own quest. Play big, play flamboyantly. Let them see you taking action on their behalf, and they will support you at every turn. This is not just true in the workplace; this is true in your family, your social circles, and your pursuit of a happy marriage and family. You want to surround yourself with people who want you to succeed.

#14: You must deal only with the truth.

Denial is for suckers and losers. You must resolve to never, ever fail to acknowledge if you have a problem or are in some kind of toxic situation that is draining your very life energy. Pretending that everything is okay and that there aren't any problems, when there are, is a fool's folly. We have all done it and painfully learned that problems don't get better with time. If there is a problem festering in any part of your life, personally, professionally, romantically, socially, or family-wise, you have to acknowledge it and create an action plan for dealing with it.

If you are not going to the doctor because you are afraid you are going to hear something you don't want to hear, then you just need to "cowboy up," as we say in Texas, and go deal with it. Look, we all know the truth when we hear it, and if you are lying to yourself, then you have an uneasy and false peace. As I said, half the solution to any problem lies in defining it. If you figure out what the problem is, then you are way down the road toward coming up with a solution.

If you are in a toxic marriage that is emotionally barren or perhaps even abusive, that circumstance will drain you dry, and that is not something you should allow to happen. If you have a relationship with a friend in which you feel as though you are being used, failing to deal with it will just drain you of important energy and build resentment that is not fair to you or the friend. Deal with the truth, and do not allow yourself to exist in toxic circumstances that will bleed you dry. You may think that you don't know what to do about a problem, and you may be right, but denying its existence is not helping. Admit that it exists, put it on your radar screen and your to-do list, and resolve to start making some progress.

#15: You must recognize and use the ego and greed of others to create a path to success.

You may remember me saying that most, if not all, people's favorite topic is themselves. That is not just an idle observation; it is powerful knowledge that you can use to your advantage in advancing yourself and your agenda in this world. I mentioned earlier that, over the years, I've observed a scary reality that we tend to believe people who like us. Think about what I just said: We tend to believe that someone is telling us the truth, not based on the validity of their message but, instead, because we feel liked by them. You can use this dynamic to your advantage. If you want the acceptance and you want for your opinion or point of view to be heard and well-regarded, you can create receptivity by being sensitive to your listener's ego.

Whether you're talking about your boss or the man you're trying to get to marry you, you have resident power over their perception because you understand how to increase your credibility and persuasiveness. This may sound highly manipulative because, well, because it is. Again, I'm not telling you how the world *should* work; I am telling you how the world *does* work. I am describing human nature, and this point is just as sure as the sun coming up in the morning. This is powerful knowledge because you can use it to change the acceptability of you and your message, and possessing this knowledge can ideally inoculate you to falling prey to the reality.

I make no apology for sharing this reality with you. BAIT-ERs use this tactic to groom victims by lulling them into a false sense of security so that they may be violated, but you can use it to create acceptance and allies in support of goals that advance your agenda without victimizing anyone along the way. Again, it is the *use* of the tool, rather than its *misuse*, that I advocate here.

Planning for Battle

Sometimes, no matter how much you try to avoid painting yourself into a corner and no matter how much you've learned about yourself and the people you're dealing with, you just can't avoid entering into a conflict with them. More often than not, knowing the "Nefarious 15" and utilizing all of the new "Life Code" play-book set forth so far in this chapter, you are going to be able to avoid most head-to-head confrontations. But, and this is a signifi-cant *but*, sometimes you may find yourself in a situation where you must stand and fight, even if it is not your preference.

Again, I'm not telling you how the world should work, I am telling you how the world does work.

For example, I would never go to a restaurant and start a fist-fight. But if I am standing in the lobby and some drunk or thug or nutball starts swinging at me, guess what? I am in a fistfight at a restaurant! The same can happen to you, maybe not a fistfight, but a conflict nonetheless. It may be at work, in a social group, or in your family or intimate relationship. I'm not talking about all-out warfare, just the kind of open disagreement that we all try to avoid, because it's often unpleasant.

But conflict isn't something you should necessarily avoid just because it makes you uneasy. Maybe you find it unpleasant because you know you're not good at it. But believe me, the person you might be arguing with may or may not be any better at it than you are. Either way, if you're prepared, that person will not run right over you.

If you get into a head-to-head confrontation and you want to win, do not shoot from the hip, and do not engage just to vent your frustrations. If you want to vent, go out in the backyard by yourself and scream bloody murder, but don't get in a fight just to get over your frustrations. There is a life code for winning conflicts, and most people don't have a clue what it is. Once you do know the code, you have an incredible advantage, which is why the next section of your playbook deals with exactly that. And remember, most battles are won or lost before the fighting ever begins.

#16: You must pick your battles and never let your opponent have control.

Never put yourself in an untenable position by picking a battle that you don't need to fight and don't know with great certainty that you can win. If it is a fight that can't be won, it is a battle that you should not fight. Life is a marathon, not a sprint, and sometimes you just play a delaying game and stay afloat until conditions change. And be careful where you shine and when you shine—timing is everything. Let your opponents think you're on their side until you are ready to declare otherwise. The element of surprise can be one of the most powerful in your arsenal. Learn how to "be" one of them, as far as they know. And when you do decide to step up and claim your position, make certain you do not outshine your boss or your mate or make his or her life more difficult with your position.

You must be clear about what constitutes a win.

If, however, it's a battle that you cannot avoid, need to win, and believe that you can, then you need a well-thought-out plan, just as you did with your overall life strategy. This time it's a battle plan. I cannot emphasize this point enough.

You must be clear about what constitutes a win. First and foremost, you must have absolute clarity on exactly what a win will look like and be comprised of. Do not ever get into a fight where you can't even recognize victory when you have it. If you can't articulate what winning will look like, sound like, and be comprised of, you are not ready to fight.

Think about it this way: If I sent you out with an assignment to find a specific house but I didn't tell you that it was located at 17 Elm Street in Chicago, Illinois, you could be standing right in front of 17 Elm Street in Chicago, Illinois, and not know you had arrived. Or you could wander aimlessly for years and not even know if you were getting warm.

You must make every effort to control the time, place (public or private), and modality of the confrontation.

The same thing could happen in a confrontation. You could be getting exactly what you really want, but if you don't know what that is, you could fight right on through it. Do you want: Specific change? An apology? Compensation? Acknowledgment? Annihilation of the opponent? Know exactly what you want, or do not begin your quest.

You must make every effort to control the time, place (public or private), and modality of the confrontation. For example, you may want it to be face-to-face, or you may prefer to do it in writing. You may choose to have others present as witnesses, or you may want to do a one-on-one. Resist with great zeal being pulled into a situation or circumstance where you are uncomfortable, because the environment can determine the outcome. If need be, be patient. Bide your time until you get your "ducks in a row" and are ready to have a showdown when and where it is best for you. Be selfish here. If you are in a battle, that means you are being attacked. Fight for you.

You must, once engaged, play to win and win decisively. It is important to avoid outright conflict if at all possible. Even the victors in battle often pay a high price. However, once you choose to do battle, do not stop until victory is complete. You want to drive your position all the way home, so there is no question that you have won or that you were right and must be acknowledged. However, it is always best to give your opponent a "face-saving" way out of the conflict. Allow your opponent to retreat with dignity—but only when, if, and after you and your position have been fully and unequivocally acknowledged. You have avoided the conflict as long as possible, you have exhausted alternatives to battle, but once drawn in, you must seek to crush the opposition. You can't be "sort of" in a battle any more than you can be "sort of" pregnant.

> ### *You must, once engaged, play to win and win decisively.*

It is imperative that you not be placated or distracted by a defeated opponent telling you what you want to hear in order to dissuade you from completing your drive for total victory.

In the field of animal psychology, there is a concept called instinctual drift: Although animals can be trained to behave at odds with their natural programming, they will, given time and circumstance, return to their genetics. That is why lion tamers get eaten by lions and bear trainers get crushed by bears. Opponents can be much the same. They may capitulate *while* you are talking to them, *while* you are in front of them, but they are very likely to "drift" back to passionately held opposing positions, given time and circumstance. That is why, once battle lines are drawn, there is often no coexistence possible and the "cancer" must be completely removed, and removed permanently. Sometimes that can mean changed lives or lost jobs, but a partial victory or resolution will come back to bite you every time. It's another reason head-to-head conflict should be an absolute last resort.

You must know your opponent's hot buttons. All competition, whether in sports or in real life, is, at some level, both mental and emotional. From the beginning of time, competitors and combatants have understood the value of knowing the opponent and getting "inside their head." In World War II, the Japanese used the radio personality "Tokyo Rose" to influence American soldiers by playing the music they loved coupled with messages to create doubt about the morality of their mission. Mental and emotional manipulation is a powerful tool that will be used either by you or against you (or both) in all competition. You may think it is unfair or beneath you and that it shouldn't happen, but it does—so you need to know about it. What you do with the knowledge is up to you.

You must know your opponent's hot buttons.

Whatever your area of conflict, I can promise you there will be something about which your opponent feels vulnerable or defensive or sensitive. A competitive advantage can be had by identifying and focusing on those insecurities. You see it every single time you watch the political debates such as we just watched between President Obama and Governor Romney. Choosing to press on these pressure points can greatly compromise your opponent's ability to advance their agenda due to distraction and feelings of unease. If, for example, you feel you are being overworked and disrespected and if you also know your boss is sensitive about the fact that the men in the office are paid a higher salary for identical work, you may want to frame portions of your arguments or demands in a way that includes that issue even if it is not your key focus. If someone you know is after your significant other and she is sensitive to having really thin hair or feels she has really big thighs, knowing that and using that to rattle her confidence at a critical time can be the difference between convincing her to move on and leave you and yours alone or not. Seriously, as petty as that sounds, I'm just telling you how it works. If that woman is after your man and you let slip or even casually comment on how he *hates* those traits, her confidence can be shaken to the point of withdrawal.

You must do your homework and amass facts, not just opinions.

You don't want to get in a street fight and be waiting for the opening handshake when that is *not* how it is done. If you do, you will get your butt kicked.

You must do your homework and amass facts, not just opinions. I cannot overstate the importance of this point. Do your homework, and rely on verifiable and observable facts, as opposed to opinion or judgments about which reasonable folks could differ. If you express your opinion that you are being treated unfairly, your confrontation with your boss will boil down to your perception and point of view versus his or hers, and "unfairness" will be debated *ad nauseum*. If, however, you have ten factual and specific examples of how you have actually been slighted (for example, you've been passed over for promotion despite being better qualified and more experienced than people who have advanced, or you have more seniority and more responsibility but are paid less than your peers), you will present a much more persuasive case. Facts leave little room for points of view and narrow the argument or negotiation to the issues you want to focus on. Again, out-prepare the other side by gathering your facts and be thoughtful to anticipate their rebuttals because that may inform what other data you need to gather.

You must never suffer an outright defeat by admitting you are wrong. If you find yourself in a conflict and, despite your preparations, you are ambushed or something goes wrong and you're about to lose the battle, you must do something to disrupt the flow of the interaction. Change the subject, redefine the conflict, change your focus, surrender on an inconsequential point, do anything—but *do not admit that you were flat-out wrong.* Understand I am saying this in reference to someone who has drawn you into an unwanted battle. I am not talking about a spouse or a loved one (unless they have become terribly toxic).

> *You must never suffer an outright defeat by*
> *admitting you are wrong.*

I can hear your wheels turning right now: "Dr. Phil, I can't believe what you're telling me. If I'm wrong, shouldn't I be big enough to admit it?" Not in war, you shouldn't. You are under attack, and your "olive branch" will be used to whip you for the rest of your life by that person or those people. Never surrender. After the conflict is over, if you want to build a bridge back and say that you have "moved your position" or "evolved" or changed your mind or learned something new, then you can do so. But if you want to maintain power and footing in a relationship, especially with those who you do not share a bond of trust with, do not pick a battle and then lose it.

I'm sorry, but that just simply won't work—which is exactly why I'm telling you to not go off half-cocked, do not shoot from the hip, do not get into a conflict just to vent your anger or frustrations, and do not pick a fight you can't win in the first place. Violate any of those principles, and you will lose power in your relationship, socially, professionally, personally, or otherwise— power that you may never regain.

Win Without Fighting

The real key to understanding conflict, however, is knowing how to win without fighting at all. Let others have the "ugly showdowns." This means never getting pulled into interactions that are unbecoming to you. Seriously, battle is not the place to play out your frustrations. *No one* goes through a battle, a conflict, without at least getting dinged up. Therefore, every battle you can let someone else fight instead of you is just that many more battle scars you can avoid. Across time, that can become significant. Support others, encourage others, but don't always be the one who leads the charge. Generals in the army don't survive long enough to become generals by charging every machine gun nest there is.

Always consider the risk-to-reward ratio when you're picking your battles. A real-world example of this is letting your spouse take on any conflicts with your mother-in-law. You carry much more risk in this scenario than your spouse does. Your mother-in-law *has* to forgive her child—but you? Not so much. *You're* not her baby—she doesn't have to forgive you, and you might end up catching one too many daggers if you enter into a tête-à-tête with her. It's hard to unring that bell, and you could permanently damage your relationship. So let your spouse lead the crusade in a mother-in-law scenario. The point is, stay above the fray whenever you can. Remember, this life is a marathon, not a sprint, so stay focused on surviving for the long haul.

Let others have the "ugly showdowns."

This "Life Code" playbook should be something you read and reread until it becomes your nature. We all need to have a plan for life, and this is meant to be at the core of your plan for living in the real world. Master it, customize it to your own personality, and perfect its execution.

6

Taking the Mystery Out of Negotiation— and Negotiating the Non-negotiable

"We can't solve problems by using the same kind of thinking we used when we created them."

—ALBERT EINSTEIN

Everything in Your Life Is a Negotiation, So Get Used to It!

Following the new "Life Code" means creating your own experience around yourself and becoming a leader of events and circumstances, rather than a victim of them. But doing so means you have to learn how to *negotiate.* Ladies, don't slam the book down and go do something else right now! I know most of you would just as soon read a chapter on how to milk a yak than one on negotiation.

I say that because, unfortunately, many people, particularly women, have a strong aversion to negotiation. They get embarrassed by what they see as haggling or cutting deals or bargaining. My wife, Robin, runs away—I mean it—when I start negotiating to buy a house, a car, a washing machine, or anything. She is gonzo. I'm not exaggerating; she starts gathering her stuff together and heads for the door. It's kind of like, "I don't want to see the labor; just show me the baby!" It's really odd because she is so tough and smart, but this one thing just makes her really uncomfortable. I have talked to thousands of women who feel the same way. What you need to know is that women, and African-American women in particular, may wind up paying higher prices for new cars, for example, according to some scholarly studies, because dealers typically begin by quoting lower prices to Caucasian men—because they know women are willing to pay more just to avoid the pain of negotiating.

But I've always told Robin that when I go in to buy a car, the negotiation margin is calculated into the price. There's the real price, and then there's the "stupid price" that they will sure take but don't expect to get. The goal is to get somewhere in between the two. They may give me a big hug if I pay the stupid price, but right after I walk out, they'll turn to the other salesmen and say, "What an idiot!" For most people who pay too much the salesman would be wrong—it's not idiocy. It's just that some people haven't given themselves permission to ask for what they want or permission to say no when pressured and to claim the right to protect what is theirs when it comes time to divide things up. To do so is your right and your responsibility, and once you decide that it is not unbecoming or beneath you, then you will find out that you've been leaving a lot "on the table" in life by not standing up for yourself. My belief is that negotiating on behalf of yourself and those you love is quite becoming; in fact, it is required to achieve fairness and balance.

Let me just say it this way: If you have a problem with negotiating, *get over it*! See how easy that was? I wish. But, take it from me: It is okay to negotiate, especially since negotiation isn't just about buying things and giving yourself permission to do so. It isn't just for high-powered lawyers haggling with movie studios over a star's contract for that next blockbuster. It isn't just for businesspeople and politicians cutting a deal on the terms for a construction project. It isn't just for merchants bargaining with vendors or customers. And it isn't just what you do at the flea market on Sunday afternoon. If you're going to win anything in the real world, you must learn how to successfully negotiate.

Let me just say it this way:
If you have a problem with negotiating,
get over it!

Everything in your life is a negotiation. You negotiate with your children, your significant other, your in-laws, your co-workers, your boss, other mothers in your carpool, and many other people, all the time. You're engaged in some kind of negotiation practically every hour of every day. How do you get your spouse to spend some more quality time with you? (Hint: not by nagging.) How do you get your children to go to bed or clean up their rooms? (Hint: not by yelling.) How do you get that raise you deserve? (Hint: not by sitting around and hoping for it.) All of these interactions you have—and many, many more—involve some kind of negotiation, even if you don't think of it that way.

And if you timidly shrink from that reality, when it comes to people who "get it" and don't have your best interests in mind, you'll be surrendering before the fight even begins. In fact, you'll be wearing a big sign that says "I'm a pushover. Take advantage of me!"

Everything in your life is a negotiation.

You need to think about negotiation in a new way, as part of the new "Life Code." Negotiation isn't haggling; it's asserting your rights—your rights across the board for your whole life and that of your family. When it comes to what you pay for something, how your relationship is defined, how much you get paid for working, or whatever it might be, you are entitled to have a say in your life. And when you decide to get tough and you begin to express that, you have started the process of negotiation, because then you'll have some idea of how things should be and how you can get what you want when you're dealing with someone else. Think of it this way: The world and the people in it are prepared to take from you and your family that which *you allow* them to take. When you finish negotiating, I want you to have such things as money, time, peace, and safety left over for you and yours, and not always for them and theirs. Someone will get it, and I just think it should be you.

Really, the only person who can deny you is you, by being passive. How is the other person going to know what you want unless you make it clear? You're going to have to live with the marriage or the work relationship or the way your children behave (or don't) or you're going to have to pay the price, so you better be willing to negotiate and make a deal you can be at peace with. And I know for absolute certain that you like to get a good deal, or you wouldn't always be talking about getting something on "sale!" Think about it, you will wait to buy something until Thursday if you know Thursday is the day it goes on sale, right? Why is the day after Thanksgiving often the biggest retail day of the year? It's because things go *on sale.* You *want* a good deal, and all I'm saying is to not be so passive that you wait until *they* decide to give it to you, because if you don't ask, they just might not ever offer. (By the way, I'm negotiating with you right now. I'm trying to get you to "move your position" on this critically important issue.)

Negotiation isn't haggling; it's asserting your rights—your rights across the board for your whole life and that of your family.

But first, let's get some more misconceptions out of the way. Negotiation isn't about screwing the other person. You could try to get a one-sided deal where you get all the money, while the other person has to do all the work, just because they're so happy to have the privilege of hanging out with you. But if you're really honest, you know that nobody is that charming, so that's not a good deal even for you, because it isn't going to work—not long-term, it isn't. Any deal that lasts, that meets the test of time, has to prove fair to everybody involved; if not, they will bail out on you and the deal, and they will do it sooner rather than later. What you should be looking for is a deal where both sides feel like they wound up, not with 100 percent of the "good stuff," but, instead, with something they can live with. So negotiating isn't about lying or deceiving or trying to cheat someone by withholding information, because the truth will almost always come out. You'll know soon enough if that car you bought is a "lemon." In fact, that's why there are "lemon laws," which give buyers a chance to live with their purchases and return them if something is wrong.

But that's not to say that using some psychology is out of bounds. Another study I ran across found that, contrary to what many women believe, women can actually succeed at negotiations precisely because they are women. In a controlled experiment, women who used their "social charm" were able to get more than $100 off the price of a used car that a male seller had priced at $1,200.

No one has **your** *best interests at heart aside from you, so stand up for yourself!*

I have been a student of negotiation for decades. (Herb Cohen is a negotiation master, and his book *You Can Negotiate Anything* is just superb.) I negotiate every day of my life. I do it on my show, with my friends, with my family, and with those with whom I do business. And they negotiate right back!

I've had many women tell me how disappointed they feel after what they might not even realize was a negotiation with someone. (Remember, I said you're negotiating on a daily basis—with just about everyone in your life.) But they're not just disappointed in what they didn't get out of it; they're disappointed in the other person, as if that person should have had their best interests at heart during the negotiation instead of their own.

You can't go to the table expecting the person across from you to roll right over for you and then lose all faith in humanity when they don't. No one has *your* best interests at heart aside from you, so stand up for yourself! You have to realize that *you* hold the power to lead the situation and guide the other person so you don't leave feeling defeated. You can't go in being passive and put all your hope, faith, and expectations in the other person and then cry foul when you lose. That's just not how the real world works, and if you hang on to that misconception, I guarantee the disappointments will continue.

I'm going to share some of the strategic steps I personally go through when I negotiate, in at least a rough order. You should consider these your new rules of negotiation so you can feel prepared—and pretty soon, you might just start to enjoy this process.

Strategic Step 1: When I enter a negotiation, I always try to "out-fair" the other side.

I don't want to have to cross the street a year from now if I see someone coming because I "put the britches on them" in a deal we made. Life is too short, and negotiating is not about cheating someone.

Strategic Step 2: I always look first at what *they* want.

Seriously, I do. It's not because I am some grandiose benefactor. I do it because to the extent I can find a way for them to get more of what *they* want, they are going to be much more inclined to give me more of what *I* want. You will be amazed how often you think you both want the same things, when in fact you don't at all. Negotiation is about give-and-take, and leaders find a way to compromise so everyone involved gets at least some of what they want and need. You're being a leader and actually helping them if you can figure out what they really want, even if they're not quite sure themselves. At the same time, I always work really hard to honestly figure out and label precisely what it is that *I* really want, because oftentimes, after giving it some thought, what I initially thought I wanted and what I really wanted turned out to be two different things.

What you negotiated for in your marriage, as a newlywed, is very likely obsolete before too very long, because both of you changed, ideally for the better, but, either way, you have evolved.

And it's also important to recognize that negotiation is an ongoing process because life is an evolution of people, circumstances, and objectives. Life is ever-changing, and so too must be your arrangements. This is why, just as you learned in the previous chapter, ultimatums don't work, because you want to keep your options open so that when the winds of change blow through your life, you have the flexibility to bend to a new reality. Even contracts sometimes need to be renegotiated. What you negotiated for in your marriage, as a newlywed, is very likely obsolete before too very long, because both of you changed, ideally for the better, but, either way, you have evolved. Renegotiating a deal is not the same as reneging on a commitment if both sides ultimately agree to make a change. Just know that, especially in ongoing situations like a relationship with a spouse or children, negotiations never stop, because the changes never stop.

Let's Make a Deal

Strategic Step 3: I always do my homework before I start negotiating.

As I said earlier, women typically pay more for the things they buy than men do, and African-American women pay even more than women in general. It's just incredible. An African-American woman could pay $500 more for a car than a Caucasian man pays, according to one scholarly study. She would never pay that amount *if* she knew they were offering it to him for substantially less. This is why you need to do your research before you start talking. If you want to buy a used car for your 16-year-old to drive to school and work, you have to start with research-based parameters. Decide on a category of car and establish the criteria you want. Say you want to buy a five-year-old compact with 30,000 miles or less. You have to start by finding out the average selling price. Do your homework; there are plenty of sites to check on the Web. With those markers in your mind, you should be able to say you're willing to pay no more than, say, $12,000 and settle for no less than a certain measure of quality. Because you've done your research, you'll know whether those are reasonable expectations before you even go to the car dealer's lot.

Strategic Step 4: Know your boundaries and limits.

If you don't trust yourself to be a good negotiator, at least do your research and set your parameters firmly ahead of time. Tell yourself, "I will not pay more than $12,000, I will not take something older than five years, and I will not accept something that has damage history or more than 30,000 miles on it."

If you do that, you won't care if the salesman is a nice guy or if the car was owned by a little old lady who only drove to the store and back, or whatever. Because you can just say to yourself, "I decided ahead of time (before I was under pressure to buy) what I want in a car and what I'm paying, and I'm not going to pay any more than that for anything less than I need." If you know that, then you've anchored yourself pretty well. This is important: Deciding ahead of time what you're willing to pay protects you against impulse. Don't decide *after* you get there. Otherwise, you'll be reacting to advertising, salesmanship, and psychological pressure, and that's where you get in trouble. Remember, there's a whole marketing machine out there that is pressuring and manipulating you in all kinds of ways to make decisions that are not necessarily in your best interest.

You'll find out soon enough if you're being realistic in your expectations. If you look for 30 days and you can't find a car that fits your category and meets your criteria, then you'll have to modify them. You'll say to yourself, "Well, okay, I'm going to have to take something six years old, or I'm going to have to pay $12,500."

Trust me, it's okay *not* to be a sucker. In fact, it's *more* than okay—that's the only way to protect yourself and your interests. But let's be clear about one thing: I'm *not* telling you to behave like a predator. I'm *not* saying you should try to take advantage of people. I'm *not* trying to teach you how to screw people over. In teaching you how to "cut a deal," I'm *not* telling you to cut the other party's throat.

Strategic Step 5: Understand people's "currency."

In Strategic Step 2, we dealt with figuring out a way to give the other side as much of what they want as possible. So how do you do that? For a negotiation to be successful, you have to understand the *currency* that the other side values. You have to know what's *really* important to them and to yourself.

There are multiple forms of currency. There's monetary currency, of course—that's obvious. But there's also social currency and emotional currency. And you need to find out what the person you're negotiating with *really* values and wants. I said that it may look like you both value and want the same thing when you really don't. If you both want the same thing, it is harder, but not impossible, to compromise or give them what you want to keep. But if you can figure out how that isn't necessarily the case, then you can be a leader and guide the negotiation out of an apparent impasse. Remember, think of negotiation as synonymous with compromise, not confrontation. Anybody can butt heads, but it takes a leader to lead.

For example, if your teenage son wants to stay out until 2 a.m. and you want him to come home at midnight, you're going to reach an impasse pretty quickly when you start demanding a midnight curfew and he starts insisting that's too early. Of course, you could always "compromise" on, say, 1 a.m. But I'll bet that wouldn't make either one of you happy.

> *Anybody can butt heads, but it takes a*
> *leader to lead.*

Instead, I want you to step back and ask yourself what you both really want. Does it really matter what the clock says when he walks in, or are the stakes much different and much higher? With parents, what usually matters is safety, not time, although it is time that becomes the battleground. If you think about it, you'll probably say something like this: "I don't want him out at

1:30 in the morning; there's nothing he can get into at 1:30 but trouble. The bars let out at 1 a.m., so there are more drunk drivers on the road at 1:30 than at any other time. I just don't feel it's safe for him to be out there." So, what you *really* want is to know that he's safe. You may not really care whether he's home; you just want to know he's off the roads and somewhere safe. That's emotional currency, and it's what's behind your insistence on the midnight curfew. You're not *really* arguing about the curfew. What's important to you is a feeling of security about your child.

And you need to find out what the person you're negotiating with really *values and wants.*

Now, what does your son really want? What currency is valuable to him? If you could get him to step back, he'd probably say something like this: "This is my one night out with my friends. To be home at midnight, I'd have to leave at 11:30. We can't even go to a movie and out to eat and over to someone's house to hang out. Just when everyone is kicking back and relaxing, I have to leave! I don't want to spend every night at home being left out. I want to be somewhere else, and I don't want to have you tell me where I have to be at whatever hour." Okay, if you see it from his point of view, you'll understand that his currency is emotional as well. It's not the exact hour that's the issue; it's freedom that's important to him and the ability to participate.

Now you can see the point. If you just pick a little bit later time, it doesn't address the emotional currency that's important to both of you. You want the security of knowing that he's safe, and he wants the freedom to spend time out of the house with his friends. You can find a way for both of you to get what you want—this isn't a difficult compromise if you lead the discussion in the direction of what you both really want, which is *not* what the clock reads. Approaching the curfew from this standpoint shows that what you thought you were fighting about isn't really what's at stake. Your security and his freedom can be compatible. Neither one of you has to "sacrifice" everything. You've narrowed the area of your dispute, so your negotiation can proceed from the starting point of what you have in common.

> *The point is not to issue ultimatums and take uncompromising stances but to find common ground.*

Now this understanding isn't something he's going to arrive at on his own. Remember what I said about creating your own experience around yourself and becoming a leader of events and circumstances rather than a victim of them? The point is not to issue ultimatums and take uncompromising stances but to find common ground. Here's an opportunity for you to lead the negotiation instead of getting trapped in a cycle of two people making demands and each building resentment for the other. Suppose you both stick to what's really important—your security and his freedom—and you say something like this to your son: "Would you agree that by 1 a.m., you don't have to be home but you will be off the road and somewhere supervised and verifiable—at your friend's house, for example, where you let me know you'll be spending the night and you'll be answering the phone? And every third or fourth weekend, you and your friends can hang out here at our house. Would those arrangements satisfy you?"

Note that the negotiation has become about specific terms and measurable outcomes. It's not about vague terms like "coming home early" or "staying out late." It's about a specific time and a specific action—making a phone call. And with that, your negotiation can reach a closure, instead of a constant battle every weekend.

When I make this point to people, showing them they have to narrow the area of dispute, identify your different currencies, give both sides as much of what they want as possible, and arrive at a specific and measurable outcome, they always say, "Wow. That isn't so hard. I don't feel so bad negotiating like that." And this kind of negotiation can lead to agreements that build over time, starting with smaller and shorter-term agreements at the beginning and eventually leading to bigger and longer-term agreements after a period of adjustment and the earning of trust.

Enabling both of you to get what you want is the essence of negotiating with emotional integrity. It doesn't have to be about business or involve money or contracts. In fact, it's usually about interactions with people in your day-to-day life. Keep in mind that all relationships are mutually defined, as I pointed out in my book *Family First*, and the definitions you reach are the product of negotiations you conduct with each other. You may think you didn't negotiate the relationship; you just inherited it. But that's not true, since you teach people how to treat you.

And when it comes to how you want to be treated, you shouldn't—and shouldn't have to—"settle" or "compromise" your standards. In fact, you should adopt an "I won't settle" philosophy, because you're going to enter every negotiation from the standpoint of acknowledging the other person's currency and trying to satisfy their true needs and desires as much as your own. You don't want to "settle too cheap" just because you wouldn't require yourself to stand up for your rights. Making a middle-ground agreement that gets you most of what you really want is acceptable, as long as you do not trade away core elements such as your child's safety, because some things are just non-negotiable.

> *You don't want to "settle too cheap" just because you wouldn't require yourself to stand up for your rights.*

Dealing with Non-negotiable Issues

Let's talk about the non-negotiable issues. Remember, in a true negotiation, the purpose is not to hurt the other person or even to gain power. As I emphasized in *Relationship Rescue*, the number-one requirement for any successful negotiation within a relationship is safety. If either side's safety is at issue, that's non-negotiable. Nobody should put up with abuse, for example—physical or emotional. There's no "negotiating" with a bully, in the sense of accommodating his need to hurt you or your child. It's not a matter of understanding his currency, because what he wants—a feeling of dominance and a sadistic pleasure in other people's suffering—is not something you or anyone else should be giving any legitimacy to. You should never "compromise" your integrity in dealing with someone unscrupulous who's making abusive, manipulative, or unreasonable demands.

If you're confronted with someone who has a history of promoting non-negotiable needs or desires, it's okay to tell yourself that certain things are unacceptable. You will not put up with a spouse who cheats on you or a partner who abuses you or children who disrespect you. These are things you know about your own values and sensibilities. In one of my earlier books, *Relationship Rescue*, I call these "drop-dead deal-breakers." If you're faced with an abuser, get out. Get out *safely* (see DrPhil.com or NNEDV.org for suggestions on how to do that), and stay out until an objective professional tells you it is safe to return—and realize that time may or may not come. If your partner is addicted to narcotics, then you're no longer living with the person you know; you're living with an addict, and that is a deal-breaker until a professional advises differently. If you're living with a cheater or with children who are disrespectful, things have to change.

At the point that you recognize a "drop-dead deal-breaker," you have the choice of presenting what I call an "ultimatum with options." You say, "I cannot and will not continue on this path, but here's what I will do to help create change and what I will do *if things change*."

If you're faced with an abuser, get out. Get out safely.

For example, your personal values should preclude you from living with someone who is poisoning his body and brain with drugs or alcohol. But you can say you will be willing to help him get some help. You can say you will be willing to try everything reasonable, short of watching him kill himself. In cases like this, what you need to do is prepare a script in advance. From writing my monthly column in *O: The Oprah Magazine*, I've found that scripts are among the most popular and useful tools for readers facing difficult people and difficult situations. Here's an example of what you might need to say to a drug addict or alcoholic:

> You're an addict. (Insert as much incontrovertible, factual proof as you have: e.g., DUIs, overdoses, arrests, hospital-izations, drugs or drug paraphernalia found. *Facts, not opinions*.) You have to stop abusing and get professional treatment if our relationship is to continue. If you do not, then we are done here. I love you very much, which is why I cannot and will not stand by and watch you poison your-self and our relationship. If I did, I would be contributing to your demise. And I'm sorry, but I can't live with myself if I do that.
>
> You can't do this on your own, so that is not an option; we are past that. Addiction is a disease. If you had pneumonia or cancer, you wouldn't treat that on your own, and this is no different. Understand, this is a deal-breaker. You may choose to drink or drug yourself to death, and if so, that is your choice, but I will not watch it happen.
>
> But let me tell you what I *will* do. I will do any number of things. I will put you in the car right now and take you to get professional help. If we need to move to get away from your drug contacts, your dealers, and your alcoholic or drug-addicted friends, I will do whatever I can that's reasonable.
>
> This is an ultimatum but an ultimatum with options. I respect you enough to allow *you* to make the decision, but understand that every decision has consequences. It's up to you. Either you can embrace me and my options or you can embrace your drugs.

Stephen Covey said it best when he said, "Begin with the end in mind." If you are forced to deal with this harsh reality, have a plan before you intervene. If your spouse says they will do it, that they will get the help, you need to be spring-loaded to take them up on the offer! If they say no, you need to be spring-loaded in that direction as well. Do not bluff here; mean what you say and say what you mean.

Do not bluff here; mean what you say and say what you mean.

Can Negotiation Save a Marriage?

The same is true if you're dealing with an unfaithful spouse. One of the questions I get asked most frequently is "Can a marriage survive infidelity?" And the answer is yes, it *can*, but that doesn't mean it *will* or even that it *should*. It all depends on how you negotiate to move forward. You need to require some things of yourself, and you need to require some things of him.

Let me give you an example of how that would go. You have to sit down with your husband and say something along the lines of:

> Okay, when you did what you did, and then when you say it meant nothing—that it was just a passing fancy, a weak moment—it may have meant nothing to you, but you need to understand that it speaks volumes to me. Here's what your behavior says to me. It says, "I don't respect you. I don't take your thoughts and feelings into consideration when I make certain decisions." And it says to me that I simply don't count to you.

I'm telling you this because I want you to know that if you ever do this again, you will do it knowing full well the message that you're sending to me. And that will make my decision very simple then, because you will have consciously made a decision knowing that your decision said to me that I don't matter to you. So if you do that again, we'll both know what that message is. And then there won't be anything more to talk about.

Maybe you didn't think of it that way the first time, which is why I'm giving you a second chance. But I want you to know what it will mean if it happens again.

And now you have to hear me out. I need for you to understand what your behavior did to me. So I'm going to talk about this, and you're going to listen to me until I fully believe that you get it. I'm going to require myself to give a voice to my feelings long enough to be certain that you get it, because if we go forward, I have to forgive you. Because the reason I'm going through this is that I don't want this to be a life sentence for you or for me. So, I want to negotiate a really fresh start where I know you now have insight and I can, with confidence, forgive you and not punish you for this every day for the rest of your life.

You "ran this off in the ditch," and it is your job to get it out. I want to be very clear that trust is going to have to be earned back. People who have nothing to hide, hide nothing, so I will expect total transparency from you going forward. I will undoubtedly check to test your honesty, and that is my right, and I claim it. If that is too high a price to pay, I understand. If you want to be with someone else, I understand. Do what you have to do, but if you want a life with me, those are the terms. There will be no more "second chances," so if you don't want that reality, then at least tell me now. If you are willing to step up and own this, then I am willing to try.

Remember what I said earlier about negotiation being an ongoing process, because relationships evolve? Well, marriage is a constant negotiation, and the negotiation window never closes; it's always open. You may think that once you say you'll honor and obey, till death do us part, you're set for life, but you're not. After the honeymoon, you're going to change, and your spouse is going to change. After you have children, they'll make a difference in how you and your spouse relate. So will in-laws. Maybe one of you will have a job, or get a new job, that makes unanticipated demands on both of you.

You may think that once you say you'll honor and obey, till death do us part, you're set for life, but you're not.

Your relationship will always involve an ongoing series of negotiations, because frankly, with just the changing of technology, there are constantly new things that can greatly impact a marriage. When I got married more than three decades ago, there were no such things as laptops, tablets, texting, Facebook, or instant messaging. The fact that so many methods exist by which people "connect" or "hook up" means that something like "cheating," which used to seem black and white, has to be constantly redefined. Is it cheating to "friend" someone on Facebook? To text or IM them without your spouse knowing? Is it cheating to keep separate email accounts with passwords your spouse doesn't know?

That's why I say that people who have nothing to hide, hide nothing. Going forward, you both have to be an open book. You have to be a picture window. So a wife can tell her cheating husband:

> You can't have secret email accounts or Facebook accounts with private passwords. You can't get upset if I check on you from time to time, and it has to be on the table that I'm negotiating my right to do that. And if that's too intrusive to you, it's okay for you to say so. Because I'm just telling you what I need in order to go forward, and if you can give me that, I can give you a second chance. But I need things in return, and that's why this is a negotiation. So, I want to negotiate that with you, and if it works out, then great.

> And if there's any part of this that's just too high a price for you to pay, I fully understand that. But you need to understand that I cannot live with a serial cheater. If you made a mistake, we'll do the reparative things we need to do, but we need to have a better plan going forward, and these are the terms and conditions that I want from you. And if you need some things from me, then I'm all ears.

We all need to work on definitions of things that are important to us, and our negotiations should not be combat; they should be collaboration. But you need to understand that when you start this process, you must have a goal. Particularly in relationships, your goal should be that your partner understands what you feel is important. When you get into an argument, sometimes you think your goal is to win when, in fact, your goal should be to be understood. You should be saying:

> You don't have to agree with me; you just need to understand how I feel, and that will be the basis of our relationship and a measure of where we are at any given point. Because if you know how I feel and what I value and you consistently choose to behave at odds with that, that will say a lot about where we are in our relationship. And the same thing goes the other way as well, if I behave at odds with what you hold dear. But if we trust each other, trust that we love each other, trust that we have a marriage in which we're committed to a common future and to our family, we'll find ways to accommodate whatever happens, in whole or in part. Maybe some serious changes in behavior will have to be made, but that will be possible, as long as we understand what's important to the other person.

So, think about that if you're wondering whether a marriage, your marriage, could survive infidelity. Once you get over the shock and anger, what do you want to express in a negotiation to move forward? Not just to express your anger, not just to punish your spouse. If your marriage is to survive, you have to start your negotiation with the goal of being understood and giving understanding.

Of course, understanding can get sticky long before the point of infidelity. I can't tell you the number of women over the years that have told me that they don't care if they ever have sex again. Imagine you're a husband who, seven or eight years into marriage, hears your wife say, "You know what; I'm kind of done with that." Now you're in a position of forced celibacy.

What do you do? She's saying, honestly, "I really don't want to," and he's saying, "I didn't sign up for a life of celibacy." What are you going to do?

> *When you get into an argument, sometimes you think your goal is to win, when in fact your goal should be to be understood.*

Well, this is obviously a very important negotiation. The only way it can proceed is by moving in steps. A husband has to begin by saying:

> All right, my first goal is for you to just *want to want* to have sex. You don't have to actually *want* to have sex, but I would like for you to work with me so that you at least *wished* you did, if for no other reason than for me.

And the wife has to be willing to say, "Well, I don't really *want* to have sex, but I *wish* I did."

Okay, that's a starting point. If the wife can say, "I can understand why that's important to you, and I want to have a sex drive," she doesn't have to lie; she isn't going to pretend she does when she doesn't. That's something you can both work with. As long as she says she *wants to want* to, she's open to figuring out what to do. Is the problem hormonal? Is it psychological? Is it physical? Is it him? Maybe it's something about the way her husband behaves? Do they need to seek counseling?

Then both partners can agree on something: "Let's see if we can make a list of obstacles, and we can work on those things together." Despite best efforts, if you can't ever get there, then that might be a deal-breaker. But there are a lot of things you can do before you get to that point. You don't have to jump all the way from A to Z, from zero to 60, from not wanting sex at all to wanting it all the time. Negotiations can take place over time, in successive approximations. That's why I said marriage is a constant negotiation, and the negotiation window is always open.

Negotiations can take place over time, in successive approximations.

And there are lot more problems in marriages besides infidelity and sex. For instance, you might say to your husband, "I want to make sure you have a job where you're home every night." But is that what you really want? As I said in Strategic Step 2, it is critically important to figure out what you really want so you don't spend time working for what you *don't want.* Do you *really* want your husband to give up that $200,000-a-year dream job that he's worked his whole career to get? Think about it. Are you afraid he's "married" to his job? Maybe what you really want is for him to strike a different balance. Maybe you want him to spend more time with you and with your children. Or maybe you just want some more peace of mind. Maybe you want him to treat you better when you are together, so what you really want is better quality, not more quantity.

Don't make your negotiation about quitting his job when you're really negotiating about something else entirely. You need to find ways for him to keep his job and for you to get your peace of mind—that's what negotiating is about. It's not about delivering an ultimatum ("You need to quit that job!"). Be sure you're going after what you want instead of what you don't want and then going after it with a vengeance. Figure out a way. Be creative. Try this. Do that. Trade this. Take this. Give that. Be flexible.

Setting Boundaries

When you're negotiating within a marriage, you can at least hope that you're working toward a common definition of a shared goal. But when you aren't dealing with someone who has committed to spending their entire life with you based on an undying love, you can't assume there is a common goal or even a basic respect for your rights. For example, at your workplace, you might have to deal with a co-worker who you know is badmouthing you or talking behind your back or gossiping about you.

Once again, you have to decide what you want. Do you want her to stop? To let her know that *you* know? To end your relationship with her entirely? You have to figure out what is it you want before you approach her, because what you don't want is to just vent or complain. You don't want to have an argument if arguing is her comfort zone—and if she's out there spewing venom, trust me, this is her comfort zone. As I've said, when you roll with pigs, you're going to get muddy, and the pigs like it. So, decide what you're going to do and what you're after. Here is an example of how such a conversation/negotiation can go: "You need to shut your big mouth, or I'm going to sneak up and shave your head!" Whoa! Just kidding! That is probably what you *want* to say. Here is what *I* would want you to say:

> I need to share something with you, and it's really not even important that you respond, because I'm not going to get into an argument with you here. I know that you have

gone behind my back, slandered my good name, and said ugly things about me. I want you to know that I know that.

Wait, listen, please, and just don't interrupt me. Despite what you say, I know it's true; I have incontrovertible proof because I did my homework before I decided to have this conversation, and I need to share with you that what you did is *not* okay with me. I am not someone who will avoid taking steps if your behavior continues. So, you've got a clear choice here, a chance to stop what you're doing.

Please do me a favor. Write down the day, the date, and the time. That will be your reminder that I have told you that I know what you're doing and that I would deal with it if it continued. I would be cheating you if I failed to communicate to you the seriousness with which I regard this inappropriate behavior or the passion with which I will pursue remedy if it continues. In any event, you can say what you want, but when I walk away, you will know that I know and that I intend to hold you accountable if it continues. You do whatever you feel is in your best interest. I hope it doesn't continue, and best of luck to you in your life.

And don't say, "Well, I just want us to be friends." You know that's not really an option here. This doesn't mean I'm your enemy. You just need to take my name out of your vocabulary, and then we'll both move on parallel tracks and not have a problem at all. And I hope that's what you choose to do. But if you don't, understand that every choice comes with consequences.

I appreciate your time and thank you.

> *Notice that you haven't told them how you know, you haven't told them what you're going to do, and you haven't told them what the consequences will be.*

This is an example of both setting boundaries—letting people know what you're not willing to do—and telling them in the most straightforward manner what your issues are. Notice that you haven't told them how you know, you haven't told them what you're going to do, and you haven't told them what the consequences will be—because you keep your plans close to your vest (#8 of the "Sweet 16" of your new "Life Code").

Standing Up for Your Children

I have always said that, as parents, we are only as happy as our saddest child. We hurt when they hurt; we feel joy when they feel joy. Aside from serious injury or debilitating disease, I think the bane of contemporary parents would have to be bullies. It, at least, makes the short list along with drugs, alcohol, and falling in with the "wrong crowd." If your child is being bullied, it is especially difficult because your options for intervention and negotiating a peace are narrow at best. You can't deal directly with the bully, or you may then be perceived as the bully yourself, not to mention aggravate the situation and create more problems than you solve. On the other hand, you can't take a completely hands-off position, in effect saying "Kids will be kids." The world has changed since we were kids, and bullying has changed with it. Where bullying was once largely confined to the schoolyard or the bus, with the explosion of the Internet and all the social platforms where kids interact, the bullies can "follow" your child home. "Keyboard bullies" as I call them, can be extremely brutal because of the impersonal nature of the medium. The distance that technology creates makes it easier for bullies to take their abuse to extremes, completely removing feelings of empathy.

When a child is being bullied, it can be, and typically is, one of the loneliest times in his or her life. This is not the time to be a passive parent. In fact, you need to be especially dialed into your child's life in this day and time. Children often feel shame when they are being bullied. They are embarrassed that "no one likes them," they feel weak if they are being "picked on," and they may hide the realities of their lives from you, for fear that you will either judge them or "go nuts" and make it worse.

When a child is being bullied it can be, and typically is, one of the loneliest times in their life.

So how do you handle the situation and *who*, if not the bully, do you negotiate with? It begins with finding out the truth from your child (maybe they aren't really being bullied and are just overreacting, or maybe it is a brutal truth) and to convince them that you are on their side, they are not alone, and you will help them learn how to deal with the attacks. Next you might talk to the parents of the bully, and this can be delicate because, let's face it, none of us is objective about our own little "angels." Those parents might be highly defensive or in denial. Lastly, you need to engage the schoolteachers and administrators.

Rather than giving you a script, I want to outline your approach for handling this last group. Remember I said that most of our communication is transmitted through channels other than verbal ones. I bring that up here because this is a negotiation where the *tone* of your approach is critical. I know you believe your child is in pain and being hurt, *but* do not run up the schoolhouse steps like your hair is on fire, hysterically yelling and accusing school personnel of being complicit, negligent, or incompetent. Instead, you want to form a partnership with these people who do care and, quite importantly, are on the scene every day, all day, when you are not. You *want* them to be informed; you *want* them to want to help you. Bullies are devious and know how to hide their assaults from teachers' prying eyes. They very likely do not know it is happening and will appreciate properly framed information.

As I said in Strategic Step 3, do your homework. Compile facts so it is not just your child's word against the bully's. That might include pictures of bruises or scratches, damaged or destroyed personal property, text messages or email chains, witness statements, and so on. Present the evidence and make your case, all framed as a request for help with an appreciative tone for an overworked and underpaid staff. Ask how you can help from your end. Be prepared for a broad range of responses. Some will just be "all over it," while others will not. Some will say that since they don't see it and much of it happens "off campus," they can't really help. If that is the response, let them know, again in the most respectful tone, that you believe it is the school's duty to provide a safe learning environment, free from fear and intimidation. Let them know, in no uncertain terms, that you are prepared to take the issue to whatever level required to get an effective intervention—whether that means the school board, State Department of Education, or local police—or that you are prepared to hire an attorney, but that you will not accept "It's not my problem" as an answer. Nonhysterical parents armed with objective evidence have a great deal of credibility, and folks will quickly realize that you will not be "dismissed" with excuses or promises without action.

Aside from serious injury or debilitating disease, I think the bane of contemporary parents would have to be bullies.

So, how am I doing in negotiating with you about becoming an active negotiator? I hope I am making headway, because I don't want you to be the only one who doesn't "get it." I don't want you to keep accepting what life deals up rather than working to get what you want, need, and deserve. You are already a negotiator, because you simply can't live in this world and not negotiate. I just want you to be a purposeful, skilled, and committed participant in the game. Since it is happening anyway, you might as well get really good at it! I want you to understand the *new* rules and apply them to the world you live in, the *real* world, and learning to effectively negotiate means you can walk away from the table as a winner every time.

7

Parenting in the Real World

"We may not be able to prepare the future for our children, but we can at least prepare our children for the future."

—Franklin D. Roosevelt

Now it's time to talk about how the new "Life Code" applies not only to you, but also to your family and your role as a parent.

I put this chapter at the end of the book because I first needed time to show you that you do, in fact, *need* a new "Life Code" to survive and thrive in the real world of today. Your children were born into a very different world from the one you were born into and grew up in. And just as you needed an "urgent awareness" to change your understanding of how this new world affects you, now you have to learn how it affects your children and your ability to protect and nurture them. You had to gain some new insights about today's real world before you could share them with your children and change how you go about preparing them to live independently.

Now that you know about the "Evil Eight," the "Nefarious 15," and the "Sweet 16," you ideally have different points of view, a different awareness, different insights, and different understandings of the real world and what your child is going to have to deal with than you did when you started this book. Every one of these lessons can be conveyed to your children in age-appropriate ways.

When the game changes, so do the rules, and—boy, oh boy—has the game changed for your children! That means your challenges and responsibilities as a parent have changed, so your tactics, including what you have to do to prepare them to survive and succeed, have to change as well.

> *When the game changes, so do the rules, and—boy, oh boy—has the game changed for your children!*

Otherwise, as Albert Einstein said, you'll be trying to "solve problems by using the same kind of thinking we used when we created them." The lessons you were taught by your parents to prepare you to exist safely in this world are no longer sufficient.

To begin with, the family paradigm has changed radically. When I grew up, the typical family was still a working dad, a stay-at-home mom, and two or three children in a neighborhood full of intact families. Today, the divorce rate is around 40 percent, and children living with a single parent or in a blended family are common. And this creates a whole new environment of risk for children.

Did you know that, compared to a child living in what researchers refer to as an intact family:

A child with a biological mother who lives alone is *14 times more likely to suffer abuse.*

A child with a biological father who lives alone is *20 times more likely to suffer abuse.*

A child with biological parents who are cohabitating but not married is *20 times more likely to suffer abuse.*

And, most shocking of all:

A child with a biological mother who is living with a man who is not the child's father is *33 times more likely to suffer abuse.*[1]

When I've presented these statistics to audiences on my show, the reaction is incredulity. But there's more:

Children living in households with unrelated adults are nearly *50 times as likely to die of inflicted injuries* as children living with two biological parents.[2]

Children of single parents had 77 percent greater risk of being harmed by physical abuse than children living with both parents.[3]

These are statistics you probably haven't heard, and they are jaw-dropping. And this information isn't from some radical group with an agenda that's trying to make single parents look bad. They're facts from sources like the American Academy of Pediatrics.

Along with the changes in family structure, the "outside world" has changed. There was a time when people lived in

---

[1] Source: Dreamcatchers for Abused Children.

[2] Source: *Journal of the American Academy of Pediatrics*, 2005.

[3] Source: National Incidence Study.

neighborhoods, and the kids you played with were the next-door kids. And if a strange person showed up on the streets, he stuck out like a sore thumb. I grew up in a neighborhood in Oklahoma City where we could play under the streetlight until midnight in the summer because our parents knew we were just three doors away with the other kids, playing "kick the can" and stepping on crickets.

But it's completely different today. A whole corridor of risk for your children has opened up that wasn't even on the map when you were their age. We are a much more transient society. Kids don't necessarily go to the local school; they go to private schools or to public magnet schools in different districts. Parents may be divorced, so their kids live in two different neighborhoods, where they're not as well known. Because of all this, an interloper doesn't stick out as much anymore.

And people who mean harm to our children have much more access to them now than they used to. Bullies used to attack their victims on the playground, in the locker room, or on the school bus. But now, even if you take your children out of a school because they aren't safe there and send them to a school in a different neighborhood, bullies can follow your children home—through social networking sites, email, instant messaging, and Twitter. And all that name-calling and harassment will follow your children to their new school.

You may think your children are in their bedrooms doing homework, when, in fact, bullies are brutalizing them on the Internet. You may think your children are just playing video games, but if you're anything like I was until just recently, you aren't savvy enough to know that those game controllers they're holding in their hands can get them on the Internet just as easily as their laptops can.

One episode of *Dr. Phil* featured an extreme version of this kind of cyber-bullying. A woman made national news when she allegedly tormented a 7-year-old girl dying of Huntington's disease. The woman reportedly posted on Facebook photographs she had doctored to show the face of the girl, superimposed on a skull and crossbones, and the girl's mother, who died in 2009, embraced by the Grim Reaper. She reportedly said she made the pictures of the girl and her mother because of a grudge that had gotten blown out of proportion, but she now regrets the whole dispute with her neighbor.

A whole corridor of risk for your children has opened up that wasn't even on the map when you were their age.

What makes someone a bully? Are some children genetically predisposed to be a "bad seed," or are we raising a nation of bullies? More and more "girl fight" videos are being posted online. One that I saw featured four girls attacking a 12-year-old-girl for about three minutes until some neighborhood boys broke it up. What's most shocking is that these girls—all between 12 and 13 years old—supposedly weren't enemies; they were supposed to be friends! The footage was shot the day after a slumber party where they had all been hanging out together. Or were they so sinister that it was all a setup to lure the victim to the beating? Neither is a very encouraging option.

On another episode of *Dr. Phil*, I spoke to the parents of a boy who received an obscene tattoo on his buttocks from his bullies. The bully "ringleader," who was convicted and recently sent to prison, wanted to apologize to his victim. But he and his mother also wanted to "set the record straight." They both said that the victim *wanted* the tattoo! As I've said on my show many times, no matter how flat you make a pancake, it still has two sides. But in such cases as these, neither side makes me feel better about putting a child out there without serious forethought and preparation.

Are some children genetically predisposed to be a "bad seed," or are we raising a nation of bullies?

Learning About That "Funny Feeling"

So, how do we, as parents, protect our children in this rapidly changing and threatening world? I've always said that the word "parent" is both a noun and a verb. Our job as parents is, at least in part, to prepare our children for the next level of life. First, when they're in diapers and can't walk or crawl, they're totally dependent on us, and all we're doing is just helping them survive. We're teaching them to eat and drink. Then, we have to start socializing them to communicate and interact and follow instructions. We prepare them to get along with other children in kindergarten and grade school. Eventually, we help them go out into the world and negotiate the hazardous terrain.

But these days, our kids—*your* kids—are exposed to complex, intimate, adult relationships when they're only 12 or 13 years old. Worse still, they start entering into very grown-up relationships well beyond their level of maturity—and that's a real problem. Too often, kids are thrown into stages and phases of life without any preparation whatsoever. It doesn't occur to a teenage girl, for example, that she might be in a chat room or on Facebook talking to a 45-year-old registered sex offender who is "grooming" her, all the while pretending to be a teenager. Your children have the knowledge but not the *wisdom* to navigate the Web. They might know which buttons to push, but they don't know when they're being played.

And even in the "real world" instead of online, we're not the only adults in our children's lives. Since we will never be the only voice in our child's ear, we need to make absolutely certain that we are the *best* voice in their ear. Here is a hugely important question that I want you to ask yourself right now: What do you really know about the adults who you turn your children over to? Do you know what kind of upbringing your children's teachers had? How about their coaches? Scout leaders? Sunday school teachers or clergy? If that sounds blasphemous to you, it is not. We're not talking about God here; we're talking about the people you trust your children with.

Since we will never be the only voice in our child's ear, we need to make absolutely certain that we are the best voice in their ear.

Remember when I said I should've written this book a long time ago? This is one of the main reasons: I just wonder how many children would have been protected if their parents had read this book, or one like it. I wonder how many parents within the Catholic Church or those putting their children in football camps with Jerry Sandusky at Penn State University would have asked more questions or done more background checks if they had had this conversation and had been stimulated to find answers to this question: How much do you know about the people you are turning your children over to?

We have to question everything we have been taught. If it stands up to the challenge, then fine, go ahead and hang on to the thought, value, or belief. But if it doesn't withstand the challenge, then don't hesitate to abandon that old way of thinking. For example, parents typically tell their children to "mind" the adults in their life. "Don't talk back, and do what you are told."

Are you kidding me!? What are we thinking? This is truly a higher form of insanity. If you tell your child to "mind the adults" in their life, you could be feeding them to the lions. Ninety-plus percent of child molesters are known to the child! Only about 10 percent of all molestation is a product of "stranger danger." It's sad but true that the people we need to watch the closest are the ones in the best position to hurt us if they go rogue. So, the best protection you can offer your children is to teach them to self-protect. Instead of telling them to "mind the adults" and "do what you are told," you should be teaching them to listen to their instincts and telling them to pay attention to any "funny feeling" they have. This goes back to what I said to you earlier about rejecting the idea of it being appropriate to give people the benefit of the doubt. This is just another example of why that is a really bad and outdated idea.

Sometimes it can be difficult to define an abstract concept like "funny feeling" for a young child. Ask your children to think of a time when they were afraid. Maybe it was in the dark, or maybe it was on a roller coaster or a haunted house at Halloween. Ask them to recall the physical feelings they had at the time: butterflies in their stomach, sweaty palms, shivers up their spine, or whatever it was that identified that fear to them. That is what you want them to watch for and react to. Identifying physical symptoms makes this concept concrete enough for even young children to understand. Let those symptoms be the trigger for them to recognize that they are in danger.

Teach your child about boundaries, and make your communication age-appropriate. As a parent, you don't talk the same to a 5-year-old as you do to a 15-year-old. You don't need to have the "sex talk" to explain to a young child where the physical lines should be drawn. Just tell them, for example, that it's not okay for anyone to touch them where their swimsuit would cover them. Teach them to listen to their bodies and to listen to their instincts.

Sometimes it can be difficult to define an abstract concept like "funny feeling" for a young child.

It may be a sad commentary on our current society, but we need to teach our children to self-protect and not just blindly do as they're told by people. They need to learn that they have your full permission to say, "No way am I doing that, call my parents, send me to the principal, send me home, put me in detention, do whatever you have the authority to do, but I don't trust you, and I'm not doing what you're telling me to do."

If they find themselves alone with an adult and get that "funny feeling" and they need to start screaming for help, they're less likely to get stage fright if they've practiced that scenario a number of times before. We should actually rehearse it with them so they don't freeze up and fail to do what we want them to do. I mean, really, I have had kids yell and scream in their front yard with their parents. So, then if something bad happens, they can do it because "Daddy told me to scream louder," and they've done it ten times before.

They need to know that if their instincts are telling them they are in danger or if they feel uncomfortable, it is okay to go to another adult and ask for help or to just leave. For example, if a stranger pulls up beside them in a car as they are walking or riding their bike on the street, teach them to turn around and walk, ride, or run the other way, against traffic. They can take themselves out of harm's way in the first 50 feet. Teach them to make a U-turn and go back, because they're more agile than a car is.

> *It may be a sad commentary on our current society, but we need to teach our children to self-protect and not just blindly do as they're told by people.*

The most important thing is to let your children know that it's okay for them to say no. If they are wrong, they won't get in trouble. They need to know you are behind them 100 percent. Can they use this "permission" to make some excuse to get out of doing something they don't want to do? Yes, they can, and you'll have to deal with that if and when it arises. But I would rather get manipulated by my child than set them up to be an easy target for BAITERs.

Parenting in the Real World

At least for me, one measure of myself as a man, as an individual, has been how well I have parented my children. Compared to that, how much money I've made, how many awards I've won, and how many degrees I've earned are insignificant details. And it hasn't been enough for me to just "be" a parent; I had to learn how to "parent."

Protecting and nurturing your children and preparing them for the next level of their lives compel a new understanding of the responsibility of parenting. Everything your children will ever be, they are now becoming. You are raising adults, not children. You are writing on the blank slate of your children. Sure, they inherited a lot: maybe your skin color or the color of your eyes or your body type. But so much of what they will become is a function of what they learn, and so much of that is what they learn from you.

Your job is to prepare them to do well in this world when you're no longer around to help them. If you always entertain your children when they're bored, they'll never learn to entertain themselves. If you comfort them every time they cry, they'll never learn to self-soothe or take care of themselves. You have to teach your child to live without you.

This means that the best way to protect them is to teach them to protect themselves when you're not around, since you won't be there forever. After all, BAITERs are unlikely to approach your children when you are there, hovering over them. Predators will carve your child out from the herd and then take advantage of them when they're isolated.

Everything your children will ever be, they are now becoming. You are raising adults, not children.

But you have to strike a balance so your children don't see the world as a scary, hurtful, horrible place that they should fear rather than a place that must be respected and managed.

There's a difference between paranoia and healthy skepticism, between fear and awareness. Of course, there are places your children can go and places they can't go and things they can do and things they can't. For them to understand the difference, you have to prepare them by building strength and confidence within them.

The goal of all your discipline is for your children to internalize your lessons and become self-disciplined. You tell your children to brush their teeth, but sooner rather than later they should discipline themselves to brush their teeth...or get enough sleep or eat their vegetables before their dessert or do their chores or their homework. Your goal as a parent is to work yourself out of a job—to become a voice that lingers in their heads in your absence.

There's a difference between paranoia and healthy skepticism, between fear and awareness.

And the way to measure your worth and value as a parent is to ask yourself this: How well am I doing in teaching my children to value themselves, love themselves, have confidence in themselves, protect themselves, and do for themselves? And all of your teaching needs to be relevant to the world that you have now learned we live in.

Don't Cripple Your Own Children

Knowledge like this has to be learned and earned. That's why you had to read the rest of the book before you got to this chapter. If you haven't taught your children what you've learned and what they have to do to protect *themselves*, then you've cheated and crippled them. You might as well pitch them the car keys and teach them to go on red and stop on green. If you put them out in the world like that, they'll get slammed.

But preparing your children for the full-contact sport of life goes beyond just teaching that there are some evil, unfair, exploitative, dangerous people out there. It's not enough just for your children to learn how to spot BAITERs. If you don't help your children understand their tactics when approaching a social or work situation, then your children are just lambs being led to the slaughter.

Let me tell you right up front: I'm here to try to manipulate your thinking, and I think you need to manipulate your children's thinking. The difference between me and those who would manipulate you for their own evil ends is that I'm transparent about it. I'm *telling* you I want to change the way you approach things. And I'm telling you what and why. Challenge me, look things up, talk to others, but when my message rings true and can't be discounted, then act on it for you and for your family. Manipulation has a very negative connotation, but the truth is that it's one of the main ways to parent effectively. I constantly manipulated my two sons when they were growing up. I manipulated them to get better grades or to practice basketball harder. I set up a rewards system, I incentivized them, and that's what manipulation is. Rewarding to encourage behavior and punishing to discourage it are forms of manipulation. It's a way of making that connection between cause and effect, between effort and reward, and between action and consequence, which children must learn to participate effectively in the world.

"Thank God you manipulated me," my son Jay tells me now, "because otherwise I wouldn't have gotten into college. I wouldn't have gone to law school, and I wouldn't be doing what I'm doing today."

I also encouraged my boys to be psychologically-minded, whether in sports or with a teacher. I would try to teach them to ask themselves questions about what was going on. When they'd say, "This teacher is just being really rude to me," I'd always ask why. They would say, "I don't know; I haven't done anything wrong!" And I would say, "Okay, but out of everybody there, why you?"

I'm here to try to manipulate your thinking, and I think you need to manipulate your children's thinking.

I was trying to get them to see things from the teacher's point of view. "Well, I don't know what she wants," they would say. "I hate that class." So I'd ask, "Well, does she hate it?" And they'd say, "Well, no, I mean, okay, it's her job." Then I'd say, "So, you hate her life's work? How do you think that makes her feel?" I would try to just gently walk them along the path of asking themselves questions to see other people's points of view.

Eventually, we'd get to the point where they'd say, "Well, she probably feels like I'm putting down what she does for a living because I don't take it seriously. But I'm not going to pretend I like it when I don't." I'd agree with that and then add, "But you can respect the fact that this is important to her, and, you know, if you disrespect *it*, you're disrespecting *her*, and she has power over *you*."

Now, when children think through things like that with their parents, pretty soon they'll be psychologically-minded. Step by step, they understand that life is more than simple hydraulics; personalities and politics come into play, and self-interest is a factor.

Remember what you learned in Chapter 6 about negotiation? Your children need to learn the same skills. Your children have to recognize that, just as they have self-interest, other people do, too. Getting along in the world involves understanding how to align your interests with someone else's. That's what negotiation is all about; that's how business deals succeed. You're both going to do a whole lot better if everybody is "eating out of the same platter."

Your children have to recognize that, just as they have self-interest, other people do, too.

I would always tell my boys that if a deal isn't fair, it's not going to work long-term. Sure, you can always try to convince somebody to do something, and they might even agree just because they like you. "Okay, here's the deal, you do all the work, and I get all the money"—that's a heck of a deal, right? Well, no, not really, because it's not going to take the other party very long to say, "Wait a minute, I'm doing all the work, and you're getting all the money? That's not okay." If you want some longevity, then you need to make sure everyone is getting something out of the deal, whether it's in business or in a personal relationship.

The same is true of when you negotiate with your children. Remember #16 of the "Sweet 16?" You must pick your battles and never let your opponent have control. This is particularly true when it comes to those inevitable battles with your children.

When my sons were growing up, I never picked any battles over fashion because, ultimately, what they wore didn't matter. It's just not worth it to have a knock-down-drag-out battle over pants hanging halfway down your son's butt. If you have a daughter and you don't like her style, get over it. Now, if her style has crossed the line into being provocative and inappropriately suggestive, that's a battle you want to choose, especially if she's way too young to appreciate what her appearance signals. But if you just don't like the fact that she wears layers, nine different colors, socks that don't match, or something that you think makes her look homeless, you know what? She can always change her fashion (and, as a teenager, she will, believe me), so why would you pick that battle?

You must pick your battles and never let your opponent have control.

Save your energy for the battles that matter. If she's 15 and wants to move in with a 27-year-old guy, that's a battle you pick. If she's doing drugs, that's a battle you pick. But how about tattoos? I realize children belong to a different generation now. Thugs got tattoos when we were kids, but now everybody gets tattoos. They were just tattoos for us, but for them, they're "body art." So, when my son Jordan wanted to get a tattoo, I negotiated with him. I said, "I'll tell you what, get a tattoo; just don't get one that you can't cover up with a T-shirt." So, he has several now, but if he has to cover them up in order to avoid someone drawing the wrong conclusion, all he has to do is wear a T-shirt.

Drawing a line like this is important because kids often don't have the foresight to recognize the potential downside of their (often impulsive) acts.

My older son, Jay, was very preppy as a teenager. He'd always dress super-sharp, his hair was always perfect, and his car was always neat and clean. My younger son, Jordan, was (and is) very creative. He's a musician, and he would want to dye his hair black with blue polka dots all over his head—I'm serious, blue polka dots. Then he would want to get a Mohawk, and he used to look at my balding head and say to me, "Dad, you have a reverse Mohawk, so why can't I have a Mohawk?"

But you know what? As much as I didn't like his hairstyles, I never picked that battle. You know why? You can wash it out or shave it off. It doesn't matter how stupid your kid gets in the moment—if you just wait a little while, it'll pass. Sure enough, one day Jordan would have jet black hair with blue polka dots in it, and ten days or two weeks later he'd just buzz it all off. Then he would grow it into a Mohawk, and then a couple weeks later that would be gone and something else would take its place.

I'm not saying you have to go along with everything your children want, but choose the things that don't lead to permanent damage or risk.

I never picked that battle because it didn't matter. And you, too, should learn to roll with it and actually get involved in it; you'll be amazed how much that will mean to your child. When Jordan wanted to dye his hair, Robin would get her hair stylist to come over and do it for him and cut designs in his hair. I'm telling you, they would laugh till they wanted to pee, and you could see what it meant to Jordan that, instead of rolling our eyes and judging, Robin and I just went with the flow. And now, he's about to graduate from USC and is a successful musician and could not be happier, and we couldn't be more proud.

I'm not saying you have to go along with everything your children want, but choose the things that don't lead to permanent damage or risk. And you could actually create a bonding experience along the way.

"Drop-Dead Deal-Breakers" for Your Children

Of course, there are some things you just can't ever stand by and let your kids do, like drugs or sex at too early of an age. Neuroscience now tells us that the brain does not reach maturity until around age 25; before then, your children's neo-cortex hasn't developed enough to enable adult reasoning. Teenagers can't "see around corners," so it's up to you to protect them from themselves and their instincts. You have to be the one to tell them not to burn bridges and foreclose options.

Both research and 35 years of experience have taught me that one of the best strategies for doing so is to appeal to your children's self-interest. Instead of saying, "Don't do drugs because it's wrong," or "Don't have sex because it's immoral," say, "Don't do this because here's what it costs you when you do."

If you can teach your daughter to value herself enough that it would be offensive to her to be used by a boy for sex, there's a better chance you'll succeed in persuading her not to have sex than you would just by telling her it's morally wrong. Try a script like this:

> If you allow this to happen and you get pregnant, you won't be able to find that boy with both hands, you will not be

able to finish school, you will not be able to go to college, and you will not be able to do things you want to do. Your ability to go out and play and party, not to mention get an education and do all of the things you want in the future, will be greatly compromised. So, all I am saying is, love yourself enough to say "yes" to yourself and "no" to him. Love yourself enough that you're willing to tell him, "You know what? I've got real plans in my life, and I'm not going to jeopardize them just to entertain you. I'm just not going to do it, and I love myself enough that I won't be used in that way. If you loved me as you say you do, you would not be willing to put me at risk to satisfy your needs."

Remember what you learned about different people's "currency?" Your children need to learn the same lessons. For example, your daughter should realize that what her boyfriend wants is to have sex with her. But what she should want is to keep control of her life. Once she realizes that, she can say, "We're not going to do that. Let's negotiate for something else."

Teenagers "can't see around corners,"
so it's up to you to protect them from themselves
and their instincts.

The same is true if your child is in danger of being in an abusive relationship or involved with an addict. Help them understand that they should value themselves enough to say:

I will not let you hit me, I will not let you yell at me, or I will not let you give me toxic substances to put in my body. If I have to do those things for you to be interested in me, then goodbye. I love myself, and I'm not going to indulge you.

If you can teach your child to value themselves enough to say that, then you're going to have a lot better chance of getting them to have some boundaries they simply won't cross than you would by just lecturing and nagging them. Remember what you learned about "drop-dead deal-breakers?" Your children need to draw the same lines when it comes to self-protection. Just as you did, your children have to understand that if they're faced with an abuser, they need to get out.

It isn't just physical abuse. Just as you learned in Chapter 6, your children need to learn that if a relationship is not two-way, if it's always them doing things for someone else, it won't work. It has to be two-way. You need to teach your children this: If the other person has nothing to offer you, never does anything for you, can never meet your needs, or you can't ever rely on them for anything, you are in a one-way relationship.

Just as you did, your children have to understand that if they're faced with an abuser, they need to get out.

Again, as a parent, you have to appeal to your children's self-interest. Teach them to be their own best friend, to be selfish on their own behalf, and to advance their own ball. As I was raising my boys and teaching them to be psychologically-minded and to be smart about it, pretty soon they started to internalize the mind-set and then generalize it to a variety of situations. Isn't that the ultimate goal of all discipline?

Now I'm a grandfather, and I'm learning some lessons about parenting all over again. And some of them are coming from my son, Jay. He was a teenager when I wrote my first book, *Life Strategies*, and he wrote a spin-off called *Life Strategies for Teens* that became a best seller when he was still in high school. In it, he said two things that are still relevant here.

When I first read his manuscript, I came across this line: "Parents, you need to talk to your children about things that don't matter." And, I thought that didn't make sense. It had to be a typo. After all, as a parent, you need to talk to your children about things that *do* matter, right? But Jay went on to explain, "Because that's going to open up the channel for when it's time to talk about things that do." What Jay meant was that parents should be talking to their children about sports, music, fashion, or whatever their children want to talk about, even if it strikes parents as trivial or a passing interest. Just keeping an open channel of communication meant that talking would be possible later, when it's time to discuss things that do matter.

Now I'm a grandfather, and I'm learning some lessons about parenting all over again.

His point makes sense if you think of an analogy. If you've ever been in an emergency room, or even seen one on TV or in a movie, you know the first thing someone yells is "Get me an IV!" They stick a needle into a vein and get some saline flowing from a bag. The point is to be ready for whatever happens so they don't have to try to insert a needle when the patient is thrashing around or in a Code Red. Likewise, if the first time you try to talk with your children is when they have something difficult to talk about, you may have a tough time getting a conversation going. It's better to have an open channel ready and waiting.

Remember, there are a lot of things that children can be ashamed of and find really hard to talk about, such as being bullied or teased or made fun of or being cast out, isolated, or excluded. *You* know it's not their fault, but to children, the message is "Nobody likes me." They feel like the bottom line is that they're losers. They're also afraid you'll make it worse (by "tattling" to the principal of their school or other authorities).

This can be the loneliest moment in your children's lives. Never take the view that "kids will be kids" and that things will just "work out." You're absolutely wrong; they won't, and that's why I outlined some ways in Chapter 6 that you can deal with authorities.

But the point here is to talk with your children first, before any next step is taken. Jay also made some good points in his book about how to talk to children about difficult subjects like this. For example, in his book, he talked to two groups of kids—one that used drugs and alcohol and one that didn't. He asked the kids who were on drugs why they used them. "I'm not judging you," he told them. "Your parents won't know. This is all anonymous." And the most consistent reason he got was that they had no reason *not* to use drugs or alcohol. For them, the question wasn't "why" but "why not?"

That didn't make a lot of sense to Jay until he asked the kids who weren't users why they weren't. He expected a high moral factor in their answers: "It's wrong," "My parents taught me better," or something like that. But that's not what they said. They didn't say it was wrong, and they didn't judge people who were users. Instead, they said using drugs just didn't fit into their plan. They just said things like, "Look, I want a car, and to get a car, I have to have a job, and to have a job, I can't be doping around." They did it because they wanted to be on the basketball team or the debate team or something like that. They had things in their lives that they were passionate about and that were more important to them than doing drugs.

Remember, kids want what they want, when they want it, and they want it right now. So, right now, they want to be on the debate team, to be on the basketball team, and to get their driver's license. Since things like that are more important to them than using drugs, parents need to make sure their children are in pursuit of some goal that makes the use of drugs counterproductive. You need to give them a reason *not* to do drugs besides just the fact that it's wrong. Help them find something to be passionate about. If they're not moving toward something like that, then they're much more susceptible to doing something nonproductive, like drugs.

Remember, kids want what they want, when they
want it, and they want it right now.

Jay taught me something else about a kid's point of view. He said, "Sometimes you parents move us forward, and sometimes you just contain us. Sometimes, it's a victory if you just help me get through my sophomore year without self-destructing. That's okay, because hopefully the next year you can actually get me to move toward something." And if they don't already have a passion, you need to help them find one. I thought that was pretty insightful for a 17-year-old!

WARNING SIGNS THAT YOUR CHILD IS BEING BULLIED

- Pattern of withdrawal, shame, fearfulness
- Onset of depression, anxiety, low self-esteem
- Persistent, vague, unexplained physical complaints
- Damaged or missing belongings
- Unexplained bruises or injuries
- Diminished social contacts
- Excuses to avoid school; decline in grades
- Trouble sleeping or eating

WARNING SIGNS THAT YOUR CHILD IS A BULLY[4]

- Angers easily
- Demonstrates a need to dominate
- Acts out impulsively
- Lacks empathy toward others
- Defiant toward adults
- Aggressive behavior
- Has unexplained belongings
- Makes hypercritical remarks about other students

---

[4]"School Bullying is Nothing New, But Psychologists Identify New Ways to Prevent It," American Psychological Association, *Research in Action*.

WARNING SIGNS THAT YOUR CHILD IS USING DRUGS OR ALCOHOL

- Rapid loss of weight
- Paleness of the skin
- Discoloration
- Dark circles under the eyes
- Shaky hands
- Dropping grades
- More absences from school than you know about
- Sudden mood changes
- Rise in anger at family members

Teaching by Example

But parents need to do more for their children than just talk to them. The biggest influence on a child's development is the behavior of the same-sex parent. And the lessons they learn from watching how their parents behave, for good or ill, will last them a lifetime.

Remember that "stranger danger" accounts for only 10 percent of child abuse. Ninety percent results from people who parents bring into their children's life or who are already there. Think back to #1 of the "Nefarious 15." BAITERs *infiltrate your life, seducing you with promises and flattery.* We've already talked about how they "groom" and isolate potential victims and infiltrate your family. Recall that shocking statistic: A child is *33 times more likely to suffer abuse* with a biological mother who is living with a man who is not the child's father.

So, you need to look at all the risks factors facing your children. What are the risk factors that the world brings to the situation? What are the risk factors that your family structure brings? What are the risk factors that *you* bring to the situation? If you're a single mother, it's pretty clear to me. You do *not* have a right to have your boyfriend move in with you. You *absolutely, unequivocally* should not have a man living in your house. You are putting your child at risk. I don't care who it is. You may say, "Oh, but he's the exception. I know him." No, you don't. And you don't know his friends. You don't know his relatives. So, you have to step back and say, "Wow. I'm a single parent, and if I let my boyfriend move in with me, my child goes from high risk to *ultra*-high risk of being victimized." *And you simply do not have the right to do that.* That is a sacrifice you must make. You could be living with someone who could victimize your child or put your child in harm's way indirectly. Maybe *he's* not a BAITER, but what about his drinking buddies? His cousin, whom you've never met? Or people who might come around that your boyfriend does not even know because they are the friend of a friend? Remember, your primary responsibility is to protect, nurture, and prepare your children for their lives as adults.

Living Your Legacy

As a parent, you need to examine your legacy. All families have legacies. What was passed on to you, and what are you passing along to your children? What are your family values, practices, strengths, weaknesses, dysfunctions? They all tend to be passed on from generation to generation until somebody makes a conscious decision to change. So, if you have a legacy of abuse, molestation, or alcohol or drug addiction, you have to make a conscious decision to break that generational pass-through. You need to ask yourself what you experienced as a child that you don't want to pass on to your children, as well as what you have to do in order to make sure that you don't.

The biggest influence on a child's development is the behavior of the same-sex parent.

Start by acknowledging that you are at risk, that you are a "carrier," or that you learned what you live and you are at risk of teaching your children what you lived. Acknowledge what could contaminate your children so that you can deal with it before they start forming relationships, getting married, and having children. Seriously, are you a "BAITER parent?" Are you one of those parents who maybe was too young when you had children? Are you relationship-dependent to the point that you fear being alone and rotate partners in and out of your life, and therefore the lives of your children, creating confusion and modeling bad behavior? Do you drink too much or mess around with drugs? Are you putting your wants, needs, and desires ahead of what is in your child's best interest? Are you fighting in front of your children or allowing them to see you being abused? If you answered "yes" to any of the above questions, then you need to have a serious talk with yourself about what your priorities are and what they should be. Maybe you were hurt as a child, and if so, I'm sorry, I really am, because no child deserves that. But, and this is a big *but*, that was then and this is now. You're the adult now and you get to choose, so choose wisely.

Stop it now. Make the decision, "This stops now. If I need professional help, I will go get it." If you can't afford it, go to your community mental health center. Go find out what the resources are, because in every community, there are resources available to you either *pro bono* or based on your ability to pay. You don't need to have insurance. You don't need to have the money for a private therapist. There are groups, support groups, parenting classes, and therapists who work on a sliding scale. Do what you have to do to stop this legacy.

> *If your life wasn't where you wanted it to be when you started reading, I hope it is getting there now.*

This needs to become a huge priority for you. And it all flies under the flag of your job to prepare your children to prosper in the real world.

Full Circle

Remember how I began this book, with a promise to help you understand *how the world really works* and *who you really are* as you go about dealing with this *real world*? Well, now you should understand why that was so important and why it required your "urgent awareness." It's only when you reach that understanding that you can pass on the right legacy to your children so they can reach a level of hard-earned understanding through your parenting.

And remember when I said I don't even want you to change who you are so much as I want to *add* to who you are? If your life wasn't where you wanted it to be when you started reading, I hope it is getting there now.

8
Conclusion

Now you know.

About the Author

"Dr. Phil" (Phillip C. McGraw, Ph.D.) is the host of America's number-one daytime talk show and is perhaps the most well-known expert in the field of psychology and human functioning in the world today. In his 16th year on television and his 11th year of the *Dr. Phil* show, he has devoted his international platform to delivering commonsense information to individuals and families seeking to improve their lives. Passionately pursuing such topics as family functioning, domestic violence, anti-bullying, addiction, and the myths of mental illness, he works tirelessly both on and off the air. Dr. Phil has carried his message from the senate chambers of Washington, D.C., to the suburbs and inner cities across America. He is the prolific author of six number-one *New York Times* best sellers, published in 39 languages with nearly 30 million copies in print. He and Robin, his wife of 38 years and counting, along with their "wonder dog," Maggie, reside in Southern California, as do his two sons, Jordan and Jay, along with daughter-in-law, Erica, and two grandchildren, Avery Elizabeth and London Phillip.